Dad,
The Difference Maker

Dad,
The Dilemma

Mama's Drama Is Because of the Daddy Dilemma!
The Fix To This Dire Problem – It's In *Daddy,*
The Divine Difference Maker!

TONY SCOTT (BARNETT)

ISBN: 979-8-9885933-4-8 (Paperback)
ISBN: 979-8-9885933-6-2 (Hardback)

For more information or permissions, please contact the author:
redeemedwriter718@gmail.com
tlmdscott2@gmail.com

Editor: This book was self-edited by the author.

Cover Design/Book Project Management:
Raindrop Creative, Inc. | StartWrite Publish Team
http://www.raindropbrand.com

DEDICATION

I've written this book with my grandson Harrison and granddaughter Rumi, who are fixed in my mind and heavy upon my heart because of this increasingly godless world they are growing up in. I also think about the great-grands that may be gifted to me after this book has been published and after I have been called home to be with our Lord and Savior, Jesus. Anticipating the birth of my first grandkids, Harrison and Rumi, even before you were conceived. I had never prayed so much for you and your parents, my sons Desmond and Mario, and their wives, Lauren and Negin, that they may lead and raise you to know and reverence the God of our Salvation – Jesus. Even so, to my children's children, great-grands, and beyond, I dedicate this book to you and your parents. To my gift from God and wife – Lisa, of *thirty-six* great years of marriage, my Ride-or-die Chick and greatest supporter, thank you! This book is also dedicated to you.

A special mention I will make of my mother, Joyce C.T. Scott, Harris. Because of your love for your children and your determination to survive, along with your faith in ***God, your Ultimate Difference Maker,*** I am able to write this book as a Difference Maker.

Thank you! You are greatly appreciated!

Table of Contents

Preface...1

Introduction 5

Chapter 1 – Our Creator Wants a Family, His Desire Is to Be Called *Daddy*...15

Chapter 2 – Disdain For Daddy, Therefore Hatred of Men 61

Chapter 3 – Why Now and The Prevalence of Such Feelings 93

Chapter 4 – Damned and Damn Daddy! 119

Chapter 5 – Daddy's Need for Their Dads 141

Chapter 6 – Let's Talk DNA – Let the DNA Talk 159

Chapter 7 – A Mother's Nightmare! 181

Chapter 8 – A Picture of Dad, a Difference Maker 197

Preface

This book, "Dad, The Difference Maker – Dad, The Dilemma," is the follow-up to my book, *"Not What I Wanted Nevertheless Everything That I Needed."* In that book, I broadly addressed relational matters: God the Creator's relationship with His creation, His heavenly host, and His crowning glory, mankind, you, and I. I had been married for approximately *twenty-five years* when I began writing my first book. I had been a licensed preacher of *The Good News, or Gospel of Jesus*, for about three years less than my marriage. And I, with the assistance of my wife, had raised our two sons to be productive citizens and respected young men.

During this season of my life, I matured as a man of God, a Dad, and even a Difference Maker; although a Dad, The Dilemma I almost became to my family. During my Christian or spiritual maturation, I began to recognize the challenges and even spiritual warfare that mightily reared up strongly against me that also opposes the family, the institution God ordained to represent Him on earth. And that I, as a man and child of God, was to shepherd, lead, and protect my family while under the instructions and guidance of the *Great Shepherd* – God my *Daddy* (Abba), *The Sovereign Difference Maker* to the lost and wayward souls of this broken and dysfunctional world.

Yes, as I emphatically noted in my previous book, my marriage had to endure a season of intense spiritual opposition and a temporary but significant Daddy Dilemma that was primarily of my making. Additionally, my family – my wife specifically and I faced spiritual or satanic assaults that targeted me and our home, our sacred space, due to my sinful nature and failures. Be it known, Satan, our adversary, has declared war against mankind – against you and me – and the purpose for which God, our Creator, made us – to display His glory. Indeed, mankind was created to glorify our *Daddy* as His imagers and ambassadors on earth. As children of God, we have been given new life through Jesus, His *Unique Son*, that like Him, we may be a light in this dark world as we also imitate God our *Daddy* as His Difference Makers here on earth: *see Isaiah 42:6,7; John 1:4,5; 8:12; 9:5 & 12:46.*

Needless to say, Satan loathes this potential and purpose intended for mankind by God, their Creator, and his offspring! The Devil or Satan, who had become a prideful megalomaniac, wanted to be like God; he was not satisfied with his position or function in His Creator's kingdom. He, having rebelled against God, lost his standing before his God and Creator in His kingdom (family) and was eternally doomed and banned from his heavenly abode, his cosmic family, and the relationship that he once lovingly shared with his Creator: *see Isaiah 14:12-15 and Ezekiel 28:12-19.*

Becoming image bearers of God is the essence of our regenerated, born-again selves – made possible through the atoning and sacrificial death of Jesus. Through His *Self-sacrifice*, we are welcomed back into the home and presence of our Heavenly Father, our Daddy. This restored relationship is precisely what Satan, in his inordinate passion and murderous aim, seeks to destroy. He works tirelessly to prevent us from becoming one with God and returning to the intimacy that existed before the fall. In his rebellion, Satan, alongside his satanic cohorts, has declared war on biblical manhood and God's divine purpose for humanity – His extended family on earth.

Men, how will you respond? Will you be a *Dad – The Difference Maker* for your homes and the kingdom of God? Will you rise up as defenders and leaders of that which God has entrusted to your care? Or will you be *Dad the Dilemma* and the leading cause of the spiritual decline and/or destruction of such homes which are to be established under God?

Satan lost his standing and role in the house or kingdom of his Creator. Real talk – therefore, he is *"Mad As Hell!* Now he once to get back at God. And so, men, he is gunning for you in particular! He knows that he can't stand against His Creator; therefore, his target has become you and me! *For Satan to get (render ineffective, subdue, or murder) the man of the house, he gets the house!"… m*eaning he gets the entire family!

Men of God, as *Dads, The Difference Makers* to this position in God our *Daddy*, we have been ordained. That we may wage warfare against all spiritual wickedness that opposes God and His family or His kingdom of Believers here on earth. Even so, through our ministry and witness, God may welcome all whom He is seeking so that He may also become their *Daddy and Sovereign Difference Maker!*

Introduction

If you have chosen to join me in this reading, having read my first book. I want to extend a heartfelt thank you to each of you for your prayers and support. For those of you who are journeying with me for the first time as you read this book, I also extend a hearty and grand thanks to each of you!

This book serves as a follow-up to my first book, *Not What I Wanted, Nevertheless, Everything That I Needed.* In that work, I take a broad approach – very broad, in fact – to explore relational dynamics and relationships in general. It examines God's relationship with His created order and humanity's relationship with the world in which we live. The central focus of that book is on humanity's relationship with God and the necessity of establishing a solid foundation in Him. Only through such a foundation can individuals, dating couples, or married couples cultivate relationships that are mutually respectful, purposeful, and victorious. This is especially true for marriages as designed by God – exclusively heterosexual covenant unions as purposed by our Creator and Heavenly Father.

As purposefully expressed in my first book and continuing the same biblical perspective in this book, it is only by embracing the truth and love of God that we are empowered by Him, through the indwelling Holy Spirit, to overcome any sinful practice. This divine empowerment enables us to break our alignment with spiritual wickedness through the redemptive and deliverance work accomplished by Jesus on Calvary's cross. In this victory, we who have died to sin and are now united with Christ are equipped to recognize, confront, and overcome the evil forces – whatever their form or whoever their agents – that seek to destroy or undermine God's creation: you, me, and our families. These wicked beings target the sacred spaces, specifically our homes, that God desires to establish with and for us as we navigate this troubled, spiritually dysfunctional world, which continually presents us with challenges and devilish dilemmas of every kind.

Although each of us, as God's imagers – both the saved and the unsaved alike – are foes of Satan and, therefore, targets of his assaults, I see the primary threat to Satan as the man or male child. Satan strategically targets God's male imagers, and while age may be of little significance to him, the younger, the better. His tactics are varied and vast, designed to effectively remove the man from God's purpose as a child of God, a shepherd, priest, protector, and provider over his home. When this happens, the family structure is greatly weakened, rendered dysfunctional, or even destroyed.

Not only does the family suffer when godly men fail to fulfill their divine roles, but society as a whole is also affected. The absence of godly men functioning as purposed by God leaves a void that disrupts His kingdom design. I reiterate what I expressed in my aforementioned book: *For Satan to get the man of the house, he, therefore, gets the house.* When a father – *Saved* and unsaved alike – fails to fulfill God's purpose, assignment, and mandate, those under his shepherding care are left vulnerable, struggling to fend for themselves without the covering and leadership God intended.

Living for God and having eternal life because of Him doesn't mean we do things perfectly or are perfect individuals… far from it! Rather, because of our *Daddy,* who is perfect in Holiness, we come to realize how flawed and broken we indeed are. Therefore, recognizing our sinful imperfections and shortcomings, we rely on God, our loving and patient *Daddy,* all the more to take us by our hand, protect, lead, and strengthen us to overcome our shortcomings, weaknesses, and brokenness caused by our sinful or fallen nature. Even so, relying on God the indwelling Holy Spirit, as we have learned to do while having patient and loving sympathy for others who are flawed and met with challenges, who we are called to do life with.

Nevertheless, when we who are godly men falter or fail before God, our *Daddy,* or those with whom we are in a relationship and accountable to and for. We, with a sincere or repentant heart, can ask for forgiveness. As we purpose within our spirit and mind to do right by the God of our Salvation and subsequently do right by others… this is the *righteousness* God requires of His children and not perfection. If we seek to do right by God, it should be easier for us to do right by all others. In this, He is well pleased.

Getting and doing things righteously or how God has decreed for mankind to live in relationship with Him is the grand theme of both books. However, it is only after one embraces a committed relationship with Jesus is when Godly righteous living or holiness is obtained. As discussed in my first book, being righteous or holy before God differs from being a so-called good or morally correct person.

A person is righteous and made holy, does good, and lives morally acceptable lives because they have entered into an obedient or submissive and loving relationship with Jesus. Apart from Jesus and His atoning blood, our good or so-called morality before God our Creator are as *filthy rags:* see Isaiah 64:6. Mankind, those who are separated from God, needs a heart change. They must be *Born Again* or *Born from Above, Renewed* or *Regenerated* by the indwelling Holy Spirit. Read the gospel of John Chapter 3.

What I will set in order to further discuss on the pages of this book is what I referred to as *The Good, The Bad, and The Ugliness* of *Relationships* as it is in my first work. Much was discussed regarding these thoughts or subjects from a relational standpoint that this book will not repeat. Therefore, I encourage you to read that life-changing book if you have not explored its pages.

In this book, however, I will zero in or narrow my focus to address primarily men, the godly or good *man.* And the messiness or ugliness of the *man* separated or attempting to make a life or do life apart from God. Here, the first mentioned man is referring to Dad – The Difference Maker! In contrast, the latter man is Dad – The Dilemma!

This *good* is that which we receive and thereby are enabled to perform when a child of God or a godly man relies on and follows the precepts and wisdom of God. Subsequently, our Father's grace, mercy, and blessing are bestowed upon such ones – those who He now refers to as His beloved, even His sons and daughters. However, this kindness and this love from God are not to be measured by what one possesses or has achieved. The ultimate reward for our obedience will be when God *restores* creation from this fallen and/or sinful order or world system. And His children then brought before Him to dwell in the presence of their *Daddy* for all eternity.

That said, obedience to God does not mean a life without struggle and sorrow… it may very well be quite the opposite for some. However, while we endure our struggles, we are to prayerfully persevere through our sorrows while maintaining faith in our *Daddy* through our hope that has been provided in His *Unique Son* – Jesus. We have, and this with prayerful patience, our hope for a brighter and better tomorrow when all things will be made new. Until that time, we must live amongst The Bad, The Ugliness, or the Dilemmas presented by this fallen world.

If you are a Christian, the goodness and love of God, our *Daddy*, should be evident in your life, reflecting the image of our Heavenly Father. However, if your story was like mine before Salvation or before maturing spiritually in the Lord, the bad and the ugly aspects of your life might have been more visible – perhaps openly displayed for all to see. Or maybe they were hidden away, expressed only in secret. Yet, God is omniscient and omnipresent; nothing, absolutely nothing, is hidden from Him. These manifestations of sin, whether outward or concealed, stem from the evil and wickedness inherited by all mankind. Living in a fallen state within a corrupt and perverse world, we were, before being born again or made new, rightfully called children of the Devil. As Jesus says in John 8:44, this was our identity before redemption.

We, therefore, before being *Born Again*, have working in us and through us death and destruction... the very work of the Devil! We were indeed our father – the Devil's children. Even after becoming saved and united with Jesus, you will find yourself warring against your old self or sinful nature. I did and do... do battle we must, each of us, keeping in subjection or under check our flesh!

This must be the aim of the child of God who is warring against their fallen nature even so the fallen satanic realm or its influences, which are like fiery arrows that are shot our way! But as I stated in my first book, *We as men must tame or euthanize that dog in us!* We must deal with the disease and sinful viral infection I termed "Dogsinitis" – that is, "Sex gone wild;" even so, "sex becoming weaponized," a perversion of God's gift for marriage. But, now utilized by Satan to destroy mankind both physically, mentally, and spiritually!

I began writing my first book during the Fall and winter of 2013. The majority of my writing occurred during these months. I completed my first draft on *July 18ᵗʰ, 2017*. However, I did not publish my book then; I didn't receive the first published copy of my baby – *Not What I Wanted Nevertheless Everything That I Needed* until *July 19ᵗʰ, 2023*. I began writing this book you are now reading on *December 1, 2023*.

What is different in the world since I first began writing over a decade ago? There are four things worth mentioning: I now have a grandson, Harrison is his name, and a granddaughter, Rumi. As far as the third thing, this has come as no surprise to me: the increased immorality in the world, in particular, sexual perversion. Lastly, I am taken aback by the widespread lies and delusions that many people now believe and woefully embrace!

What we are facing as a people is intensified spiritual warfare against the children of God; as for those who are lost to this world or Satan, they are up against satanic strongholds that can only be broken by Jesus alone! Unless the Redeemed of the Lord are prayerfully watchful and regularly in communion with Jesus, any of us can become ensnared by these strongholds – this I came to know very well when I experienced Satan's sexual trappings, resulting from my spiritual immaturity. And, at the time, unknown to me was the ability of my sinful nature or sexual proclivity to get the best of me!

I take on this matter of sexual immorality with unfettered transparency in my previous book. Prior to writing that book, I had raised two sons to become men. However, while we were parenting, my wife and I had withstood the destructive spiritual forces aimed to render me ineffective as a dad and husband and to take my wife out mentally in an attempt to overcome our marriage and our witness and praise as our *Daddy's* children. This matter is thoroughly addressed in my first work.

Assuming that you have not read that book… I was not without fault, which was the very reason why these forces and challenges came against my home. Being an immature Christian, nevertheless, a child of God, and with only *3 ½ years* into my marriage, I unknowingly and ignorantly put myself in reach of Satan's plant – a Seductress, his agent to bring me down and overtake my house. Immediately, my mind was led astray by this Seductress, and slowly, my sleeping *Dog* was aroused!

With my help, spiritual wickedness came after me full-throttle! As I've stated, Satan's target is on the back of men, even while we are yet boys; the earlier he can pervert the minds of children, the better it is for him regarding his endgame – to keep them in spiritual darkness and to ultimately lead them to utter destruction! Even so, the younger the child, the easier Satan's control over such ones is maintained, thereby rendering many helplessly ineffective for the kingdom of God because of the emotional damage and mental entrapment that Satan is ultimately behind. That said, no one is beyond the Saving Grace of Jesus… no, not one!

For Satan to conquer a male child or overtake a man – both having sinful natures and already at war with themselves, whether mentally or through their fleshly passions – the evil, as the power of darkness and master of deception, can easily seize and destroy God's design for families or individuals. With little effort, Satan can undermine, dismantle, or overthrow families during their formation or assault and overcome them even after they have been established.

The Devil also seeks to undermine God's ordained design for families through perversion and lies, including his promotion of same-sex unions and confusion about marriage. He also advances this agenda through the concept of "gender dysphoria," a notion endorsed by organizations like the American Pediatric Association (APA) and the World Health Organization (WHO). However, the Word of God unequivocally and boldly identifies such practices and behaviors as sin.

From my personal experiences and encounters with others, this book will delve into matters and details that I did not fully explore or mention in my previous work. Among these are the surprising revelations from my DNA test results, which unveiled unexpected aspects of my paternal heritage and history. This journey began to unfold on December 2, 2020, and culminated dramatically on April 7, 2022, during the Noonday. By then, my final manuscript for my initial book had been completed, with only additional editing remaining.

Initially, my sole interest in the DNA test was to trace the geographic origins of my African ancestry. However, the test results, along with a DNA match, uncovered far more than I anticipated or had even considered possible. These findings revealed a complex web of genealogical truths, shedding light on the bad, the ugly, and the brokenness of the man I've identified as my paternal progenitor.

What became more evident through this discovery was not just the brokenness of this man but the universal brokenness of humanity – brokenness that manifests most profoundly in the lives of men estranged from their Creator. When men are separated from God, they fail in their divine mandate to lead, protect, and nurture, leaving a wake of pain and disorder. Yet, even in this state of rebellion and spiritual ruin, the steadfast love of God remains. His mercy extends to the lost, and His grace calls the broken back into fellowship, offering restoration and redemption to those who will receive His love for them.

Spiritual healing and deliverance from sin, God our *Daddy* seeks to bring to His spiritually damaged, lost, and rebellious prodigal children. Meanwhile, He mercifully waits patiently with arms wide open to welcome us home. Today could be your day to return to your God, Creator, and even **Progenitor**. All you need to do is repent from your sins and acknowledge Jesus as your Lord and Savior! Jesus gave Himself over to the Cross so that you may have *Eternal Life* and *life more abundantly* no matter your past, your sins, who you are, were*, or even who you thought you were!*

It is through embracing our eternal and spiritual reality in Jesus – our *Ultimate Difference Maker* that we as men can become Dads, the Difference Makers as sons of the Most High God - Jehovah!

Because of Jesus, we are given new names and a new identity. No matter your circumstances on earth or Hell's influences that have worked against you, nothing can negate this fact!... YOU ARE A CHILD OF THE KING! In Him, you reign supreme above everything that will attempt to rob you of your identity in Jesus!

CHAPTER I

Our Creator Wants a Family
His Desire Is to Be Called *Daddy*
(Matthew 6:9)

A Brief Introduction to The Book of Genesis,
The Triune God, our Creator, and His Established
Order and Redemptive Plan

As with the opening chapter of my previous book, *"Not What I Wanted Nevertheless Everything That I Needed."* I thought it only fitting that our introduction for this companion tome also utilizes the book of Genesis as its opening and foundational reading by which we are to be illuminated. We will cover these Scriptures with different insights provided soon enough.

Genesis is the first book of the Judeo-Christian Bible, hence, the beginning of mankind's history and our origin of life – namely, our physical composition (earthen bodies) and our spiritual constitution (heavenly essence) joining and animated or wrought by the Holy Spirit (*Nishmat Chayim* and sustained by the breath or *Ruach*) of God, thereby He bringing forth unto Himself a living soul (Nephesh) or conscious and intelligent human-being – Adam (Adamah), meaning *Man* – mankind or humanity. This dual reality of *Man* or mankind was created and brought forth into being by God our *Daddy – the Triune God,* the Creator of earth and all there is (Genesis Chapters 1& 2).

Having been fashioned by God our Creator, we were made to be in communion and, as a family member with the *Divine,* to display or imitate our Father's glory. Like *Daddy,* we, His children or offspring in the spiritual sense or essence, were designed and purposed to be like Him in character and as His imagers here on earth, His bodily representative as good stewards of our earthly domain to include ourselves and others.

However, after the fall or rebellion of *Man* (Adam and Eve) against their *Daddy* and, subsequently, their and their offspring's (you and I) separation from Him – hence the death sentence was enacted by their now estranged Father – Yahweh or Jehovah (Gen. 2:16,17). Nevertheless, it was and continues to be our Creator's sole purpose throughout mankind's history to reveal Himself. Or to be made known through His redemptive love to His lost and desolate children who, because of their rejection or disobedience to their *Daddy,* were physically and also spiritually divorced or cut off from God – meaning His eternal life-giving essence – *Zoe.*

Therefore, His intimate presence no longer sustained them – they were no longer one with their *Daddy.* Hence, mankind would now be dead in their sin, subsequently united with Satan because they were no longer one with God, Who is Life or *Zoe – Eternal life.*

As a result of the Bible – the written Word of God, as a spiritual reality, our Creator and *Daddy* is seated before us; therein the Sacred Scripture, He speaks to us and makes Himself and His love for us known as we read or hear from Him through His Word – the Bible. In so doing, He shows and provides "The Way" – His Redemptive Plan for His lost and disobedient children to return home to the safety of their loving and patiently waiting *Daddy.*

Yes, our *Dad,* He wants you back home with Him, no matter the state you are in because of your sinful condition. He truly yearns for his wayward offspring – you to return to His care. And then He will begin to renew your thinking and cleanse you from your ugliness and messiness due to sin – your fallen condition. Our *Divine Dad* yearns to restore you to a right relationship with Him through Jesus. He then wants to transform your broken or sinful way of thinking. Only then can a man begin to function in their proper role before God and His designed purposed by His *Daddy* as head of their family, a sincere *Man of God,* a follower of Jesus, and Difference Maker (Luke 15:11-32; Romans 12:2).

In the initial chapters of the book Genesis, my *Daddy* set forth mankind's function and purpose that are to be perpetually established and ordered by Him. God created you and I for His set purpose: to represent Him in an orderly manner on earth as His image-bearers, even so, the children of His kingdom. We are to be His earthly families, households led by godly fathers, partners with our Creator as He gifts to a husband and wife offspring to represent their parents, even as parents are to glorify God their Father as His representatives. As imagers of our *Dad,* we demonstrate that we are His or *one with Him* as we, by the help of the Holy Spirit, purpose in our hearts and renewal of our thinking from the *Word of God,* seek to follow after Jesus, our *Elder Brother* and *Great Shepherd* (John 16:7-10; Matthew 4:4 and Luke 4:4).

God, being our heavenly Father and Creator, He alone knows what's best for us, His workmanship and children. As well… how we are to perform His will so that our lives may be lived to His standard of holiness; we, thereby, receive His best for us in this fallen world and, more importantly, His promises in the world to come – a world without end!

Furthermore, we acquire His loving counsel, as provided in the Bible, so that we are kept safe from self-imposed harm and dangers or such threats that are inevitable in this fallen, demonically influenced world of spiritually broken and even dead people! Apart from God, this is what we are – dead in our sins (Colossian 2:13). As for those of us who are now called children of God, we are to become dead to sin, no longer living after our sinful passions or patterns of this world, because we are now *kingdom children,* even imagers of God our *Daddy* (Romans 6:12-19).

Death as A Dilemma

As discussed in depth in my previous book, we observe the Serpent or Satan's seduction of Eve and her and Adam's disobedience against God's one protective and loving prohibition, *"Don't eat from the tree of the knowledge of good and evil,"* consequently their defiance leading to this world's unceasing troubles and struggles. This, their disobedience in eating from the forbidden tree, as their judgment – separation from God – *hence spiritual death* becoming our Dilemma, this being the cause of this world's suffering, sorrows, and disturbing dilemmas of all sorts of evil and woes, not the least of which our physical death – our bodies subsequent return to the earth (Genesis 2:17; Romans 5:12; 1 Corinthians 15:22).

According to Scripture, death is to be understood as separation from God in this world and for all eternity – what a Dilemma (Isaiah 59:2; Roman 6:23; Ephesians 2:12,13!

This Earth, which is soon to pass away, is merely a sojourn for the *Child of God* (1 Chronicles 29:15; Hebrews 11:13). The Earth, as with mankind, is also under the curse of death or is corrupt, resulting from the *Edenic Fall* (Genesis 3:17; Romans 8:19-23). If you are not included in this number as a *Born-again Child of God*, sadly, and to the tremendous grief of the child of God or the Redeemed's *Daddy* – your Creator is He *only*. Howbeit, not *Daddy* for the unregenerated – such ones who have not been cleansed by the redemptive blood of Jesus. Yours... for you who remain one with this fallen world, who is subsequently one with Satan, eternal abode and second home, or more aptly put, your spirit's imprisonment of eternal suffering will be in the Gehenna, where you will spend eternity – the ultimate dilemma (Matthew 5:22; Matt. 10:28; Mark 9:43-47)!

Howbeit, this place of torment was not purposed for *Man* – God's offspring but rather for the heavenly *spirit beings* or *elohim* who rebelled or committed mutiny against God, their Creator, and too, who forfeited or lost their intimate relationship and heavenly abode with their Creator (Matthew 25:41; Mark 9:43; John 1:12; John 8:44; Romans 8:15; 1 Peter 2:4; Jude 1:6; Revelation 20:10).

God Speaks to Us Through His Holy Word

The *Triune God*, who spoke or breathed forth and created life as provided in the opening chapters of the Book of Genesis, also *inspired* or *spoke* to the hearts and minds of some 40 penmen to express His love and truth to *Man* through His Holy Word – the Bible (2 Timothy 3:16,17; 2 Peter 1:22,21; John 1:1,14*)*.

These writers – all men within the Bible were either prophets, priests, kings, and apostles, with there being a few exceptions, Luke, Mark, James, Jude, and Nehemiah, whose hearts and hands God directed to write precisely, with cohesiveness, and without error or contradiction, with the Bible's earliest writings having been initially passed down through oral traditional storytelling, songs, and poetry before put to papyrus (paper) His loving and instructive Words for His creation over several hundred years.

We call this masterful and supernatural work of the *Holy Spirit*, the Holy Scripture, the very Word of God to *Man*. Maintained within the Protestant tradition are *Sixty-six* books that comprise the Old and New Testament of the Bible, which are our *Daddy's* Words to His children, as well… His teaching to those who are seeking to know the truth of God, their Creator and *Ultimate Difference Maker*.

The cohesive consistency, parallels, merging, or marrying of these historical occurrences and themes provided by these Biblical authors read together as orderly, unified, and well-constructed narratives highlighting mankind's history along with God their Creator. Yet, first and foremost, we are also provided in the Holy Writ, Jehovah, our *Daddy's* unfailing love for us, His redemptive plan for *Man*. And His intimate dealing with the ancestry of Abraham, Isaac, and Jacob through which Jesus, the Messiah, and Savior of the world, *Who* was to come. This, the *Proevangelium, or Good News of Jesus,* is first declared here in Genesis 3:15 of the Bible – our Father's *Love Diary*, instead of a *"Love Letter"* to the people of His making.

In my previous book, I described the Bible as God's "Love Letter." There's nothing wrong with this endearing description. However, by choosing to describe the Bible as God's Love Diary, I posit that this form of expressive writing suggests a depth and breadth of expression that exceeds that of a Love Letter.

God's Name Made Great through Man and His dealings with Mankind

Included in this *Diary* or Holy Scripture is also God's final judgment of *Man,* along with the rebellious angels (elohim)… this world's end, and God's kingdom, which is to come, both His millennial kingdom on earth followed by His eternal kingdom – *The New Heaven and New Earth!* Through God's union or covenant, and even spiritual marriage with this people group – the Israelites of the Old Testament account of the Bible, God first called forth and chose Abram as His own so that God's name may be made *Great* (Genesis 12:2,3; Exodus: 9:16; Malachi 1:11; John 12:28 &17:1-4).

This rendering of his name, Abram, means *exalted father,* subsequently, "Abram" giving birth or rise to the nation of Israel – the "Jewish" people in modern terminology from then the seed of "Abraham" – God's therefore rendering of Abram's new prophetic name as "Abraham" means, *father of many* (Genesis 12:1-3; Gen.17:4,5 vs. 19-21; Gen. 28:13,14 and Galatians 3:7 & 29).

To and through this divinely chosen family, also identified as Hebrews, as an expanded people group or nation – also identified as Israel, the God of creation made and makes Himself and His plans for the world known through this people and His *Diary – the Holy Word.* Even so, my *Daddy's* name being made great throughout the earth, as He called Israel His own, His chosen people. Additionally, His son, He calls them amongst other intimate descriptives, thereby expressing the familial relationship He longs to have with them. Although, as a nation and for a time, they have rejected Jesus as their King and Messiah.

Regarding making Yahweh's name great, this would have been primarily during such times when His chosen people were obedient and represented Him well, leading to His abundant blessings upon them. However, also during His judgment upon Israel and the other rebellious nations did the nations come to know God through His mighty acts.

Furthermore, our *Daddy's* name being exalted with the life and ministry of Jesus, resulting from His sinless perfection, imaging or representing His Father in His humanity and divinity – *Hypostatic Union* or *Incarnation,* has with perfection made and continues to make His Father's name **Greatly Glorified** throughout the Church age – these times set before us as the Holy Spirit continues to reveal Jesus and His work in and through the sons and daughters of Yahweh (John 5:19,20; John 14: 16,17 & 26; John 16:7). Howbeit, many continue to reject and rebel against their Creator – Jehovah, not the least of which, modern-day Israel – the Jewish people.

As we have seen, our Father's previous familial relationship with Israel and His current longing for their obedient acceptance of Him as their Creator is not limited to them alone. The Creator also longs to reclaim and restore all humanity to Himself – all His prodigal, sinfully rebellious, hopeless, and helpless children, including non-Jews (Gentiles). However, this longing does not exclude Israel, nor does it suggest that the Church replaces non-Messianic Jews who have rejected Jesus (Yeshua, meaning 'Savior') as their Messiah, the *Anointed One and preeminent Son of God* (Genesis 3:15; Isaiah 49:6; John 3:16,17; 1 Timothy 2:3,4; 2 Peter 3:9).

Acknowledging God as Daddy is Through Jesus Alone

Now, identifying God as **only** one's Creator whereby making a distinction between God as Creator with His preference also being one's lovingly relational and familial *Daddy*. Underscoring these important aspects: being permitted to call God *Daddy* and He claiming us as His child[ren] depends upon one's standing before and with Him through Jesus' self-sacrifice. Through this *Gift of His Son*, His desire is for children to call His own; in return, we are permitted to call our Creator – *Daddy*.

Even so, such ones are His adopted sons and daughters (Romans 8:14-17; Galatians 4: 4-7; Ephesians 1:5) who are to, therefore, purpose in their hearts to represent their *Daddy* as was perfectly modeled for us by Jesus, who is also our spiritual *Elder Brother* (Romans 8:29; Hebrews 2:11). Now, contrasting those who have no standing *with* Jesus, but instead, you stand *against* Him – having rejected His gift of Salvation; even so, this being a rejection of His Father and my *Daddy;* therefore, He currently stands before and against you, sorrowfully as your Creator and Judge (John 3:18 & 36; John 14:6; 1 John 5:12; 2 Thessalonians 1:8,9)!

Regarding Yahweh's name becoming world-renowned and made great throughout the then-known world, the Roman Empire, this fame of the Triune God and the spread of the Good News of Jesus occurred as described in the Book of Acts (Acts 1:8; 8:4; 13:47) and further affirmed in Colossians 1:6 and 1:23. This global renown was due to the prophetic life and self-sacrifice of Jesus, who was a Jew in body. Yet, Yahweh, the self-existent Spirit Being (Elohim), is uniquely revealed through His divine Son, Jesus. As with Yahweh, Jesus has also – indeed, has always – eternally existed as God (Elohim or Spirit), the *Sovereign Spirit-being*, co-equal with His Father.

While dwelling on earth, Jesus clothed Himself in flesh, becoming fully human as a Jew, yet He remained one with and equal to His Father. In every aspect of His earthly journey, Jesus flawlessly represented His Father – His *Daddy* – even as He took on the form of a man. Like Father, like Son, Jesus perfectly revealed the character and will of Yahweh. He was God clothed in a garb of flesh for our sanctification and ultimate reconciliation. Through His incarnation, Jesus not only revealed God's love but also became one with humanity, demonstrating how *Believers* are called to live as Difference Makers for God, their heavenly *Daddy* (John 1:1–14; John 6:38; John 17:5).

God is the Creator of all mankind, yet not all are His spiritual sons and daughters. Only those who answer His call and accept His invitation through Jesus are born again and united with Him as His children. These Born-again Believers are indwelt by the Holy Spirit, becoming members of His kingdom and partakers of His divine nature. As Jesus taught, it is through spiritual rebirth – being born of water and the Spirit – that one becomes a child of God (John 3:5–7, 16–17). This divine adoption empowers believers to live lives that glorify God and reflect His nature to the world.

Understanding the Usage of Son and Man

The wording *son* or *son* of man or *sons* of God, as utilized in the Bible, can be observed as being gender-neutral – representing both male and female as ontological equals before God, even though Yahweh has established order through the system of hierarchy within godly homes by which to function (Exodus 4:22; Romans 8:14-17; Galatians 3:26-29; Gal. 4:4-7 and Ephesians 5:22-32). Likewise, *Man,* which is a derivative of the word Adam (Adamah) – hence meaning created from the earth; therefore, all of

Earth's inhabitants can be described as *Man* – gender-neutral, as demonstrated in both of my books.

This view is illustrated in Genesis 1:26; herein, God says, "Let *us* (*Us* and *Our* is a picture of the Triune God) make *Man* in our image, after our likeness…" Such usage of *son* and *man* is evident throughout Scripture. And, therefore, not a misogynist attitude against women or patriarchal bias toward men as Satan has led many to believe the Bible promotes. This is clearly one of Satan's diabolical tactics to usurp God's purpose and authority and assignment He has appointed to godly men that they may effectively shepherd or lead their families as ordained by God our Creator.

Before creation's beginning and the reason for the created earthly realm and the fashioning of *Man*, the Triune God wanted a family to love and care for here on earth. Soon enough, He will have His restored, though not fully realized, kingdom – a family that will reign upon the earth, albeit temporarily – that is, for a millennium (Revelation 20:1-6) until He makes all things new in His restored and eternal kingdom fit for His reborn and spiritually adopted sons and daughters (2 Corinthians 5:17; Hebrews 12:25-29; Revelation 21:5).

A Picture of God's Family or Kingdom on Earth as it is in Heaven

As there are heavenly created sons of God - elohim, or heavenly beings (angels or spiritual bodies) abiding and functioning orderly within their realm and designed or purposed stations (Job 38:4-7; Psalm 82:1), so does God desire a kingdom of people, His representatives (family) *on earth as it is in heaven* performing His will – that is for His sons and daughters in obedience and love for *Daddy* to image His essence and heavenly domain during our short-stay or sojourn on earth.

This modeling, with the help of the *Indwelling Spirit* of things in heaven, is that which our Father desires for His children to give their hearts to and purpose to strive for. And it is the King's sons – godly, sanctified men who have been given authority or assignment by their *Daddy – the King,* as it is with His rule...for men – daddies and husbands to manage, rule, to display loving and sacrificial dominion over God's spiritual kingdom of sons and daughters on earth represented through individual families, as is the order of things in heaven.

Like our heavenly Father, those – men who are His sons are to be heads or good shepherds and stewards over their homes, which God has given to the care of godly husband to establish (Genesis 2:23,24 and Ephesians 5:31). People, this is a tremendous undertaking and yet an awesome and privileged responsibility assigned to fathers. A wife and mother's complementary tremendous undertaking and yet awesome and privileged responsibility assigned to her from God is to carry within her new life whom God desires to adopt into His family and embrace as His own.

Wives (mothers) who are innately nurturers are to care for their gift from God in ways that a husband (father) is incapable of. Both husbands and wives with their innate God-given opposites and yet complementary attributes. When they are one with God, following His counsel and functioning within their God-designed roles, including displaying love, caring for one another, and raising their child[ren] to reverence God their Creator, in this, our *Daddy* has great delight...in this we who are children of the Most High God, we are fulfilling our purposed assignment as imagers of our *Daddy*. Like our Daddy, so should His sons and daughter be... How are you doing with this?

We see in Genesis 3:9 that God holds Adam accountable as He calls him out for his wife's sinful rebellion along with his involvement...Why? Because Adam was created first, he was instructed by his Daddy to subdue and rule the earth with his wife alongside him; Adam was given authority to name the creatures of the earth, as well, provided by Yahweh one command – to *leave the forbidden tree alone!* These mentions exclusively to and regarding Adam and mandates from God indicate his *Daddy's* assigned purpose and God-ordained authority endowed upon him as a servant-leader. It's worth mentioning: The man, not the woman, is additionally commanded to leave his father and mother to establish **his** own home, read Ephesians 5:22-33 and 1 Timothy 3:4,5.

What's In the Name Adam?
Order In the House

Now emphasizing! This matter of *Man's* rule during the Church Age – these current times does not suggest that Christians – the Church, or the children of God are to seek to rule or attempt to establish a theocracy in this fallen world, which, through God's permissive will and judgment upon *Man* is currently under the dominion of Satan (John 12:31; John 14:30; 1 John 5:19). Instead, we, as our *Daddy's* imagers and representatives, are to be Difference Makers or godly influencers to the lost, troubled, broken and Fatherless souls of this corrupt and evil world (Luke 17:20,21; John 6:15; John 18:36). Such ones, our *Daddy* wants His reconciled and redeemed children – the Church to lead back to Him.

Having pointed out that the description or term *son of God*, etc., along with the name or title Adam (Adamah) or *Man,* is inclusive – denoting both male and female. Now, let's examine further the understanding of the name Adam as provided in Genesis 2:23,24. The name Adam, as stated, can be translated as *Man* – hence mankind or humanity. However, within the Scripture provided – Genesis 2:23,24, the Hebrew designation/description for Adam is *Ish*, and for woman, it's *Ishshah*.

Ish is the masculine Hebrew name for men, also the title husband, whereas *Ishshah* is the feminine Hebrew designation/description that derives or originates from the *male,* even so his masculine designation*, Ish.* The pictures provided in Genesis can't be more evident… God created *Man*, both male – XY Chromosome and female – XX Chromosomes, with the woman – *Ishshah,* originating from her male – *Ish* counterpart, whom God joined together as husband and wife (Genesis 2:24 "one flesh"), complimentary opposites – sexually compatible for His set design and purpose to procreate that His now or current spiritual kingdom may be expanded throughout the earth within the souls of mankind… a kingdom without boarders – hence not a Christian Nation as many who are Trump supporters are advocating for when he returns to the office as president in 2025 (Matthew 28:19,20; Acts 1:18; Luke 17:20,21; Romans 14:17; John 18:36).

That said, once again, the first *Man* created was formed male; his position as the first mentioned, the first to be created and who alone was instructed by God, is important… this cannot be understated! According to Biblical hermeneutical studies regarding the *Law of First Mention*, it sets the precedence, the meaning, and how one should be guided by the initial understanding or presentation of a text, theme, word, etc., when studying the Bible in its entirety.

Yes, Eve – the woman, and this Hebrew designation of Eve – *Chavah*, meaning to give life, was given as Adam's helper and his ontological equal. That said, and there being no Biblical change with these views, overall accountability and responsibility of a God-ordained home are to be welcomed and shouldered by a godly man – husband and father, so that there may be **Order In the House!**

Eve – *Ishshah,* female *Man* or womb-man and bride. Because she was taken from and/or created by God from the male version of *Man* and created by God as the female form of *Man* (Genesis 2:21 -23), not only was she created to represent Her Creator... she was also stationed in life and purposed by God to follow her husband's lead that she may represent him as they are being led by God, that there may be order in the house.

Eve, the second *Man* – woman or *Ishshah;* she, therefore, having been created by God from the rib of the male version of *Man,* her complementary opposite and equal, her head and home's leader as the husband; to him, she belonged; even so, to her, he belonged! Together, they were to live under God as *one* – husband and wife united or brought back together by God and accountable to one another under God's Sovereign headship until death due them part (Matthew 19:4-6; Genesis 2:22; 1 Corinthian 11:8,9; Ephesians 5:28-31).

Man, God Partners in Building His Spiritual Kingdom on Earth

Through their distinct, complementary biological differences as male and female, God perpetually, purposefully, and distinctively created sexual functions and roles for *Man* – Adam and Eve to honor and partner with our *Daddy* to His glory and their subsequent fulfillment and blessings. Even so, so that they may honor and serve one another while stewarding their *Daddy's* earthly Kingdom – His individual families as permitted by God to husbands and wives.

Additionally, enjoying the sexual pleasures gifted only to this union of a biological male–husband and biological woman–wife, God's partners in building His spiritual kingdom through procreation and populating the earth. This continues to be our Daddy's will until things are rendered complete during Jesus' *2nd Coming* with all *Believers* to establish His millennial reign and kingdom on earth (Zechariah 14:5; 1 Thessalonians 3:13; Jude 1:14,15; Revelation 19:14). Meanwhile, God's current earthly but also spiritual kingdom and family is to model heaven – Jesus Himself. And according to Scripture, God, our Father's will… being *done on earth as it is in heaven* (Matthew 6:10; John 5:19: John 14:7; John 15:8). This is now being practiced or done in part. When Jesus returns, our Daddy's will will be perfected or completed!

Together, man and woman, both male and female, were separated and distinguished by God through their internal biological design and outward earthly form, including male and female genitalia and other distinctions. In His wisdom, God created them to reflect Him as His image bearers, granting them the privilege of procreation. Like their heavenly Daddy, Adam and Eve were designed to be life-givers, entrusted with bringing forth and nurturing new life. Just as God is the eternal source and sustainer of life, He purposed mankind to partner with Him in the sacred role of life bearers, mirroring His creative power and love. Yes, like God our *Father*, alike, with limitations are his sons and daughters.

For *Man,* this is perhaps their greatest gift and purpose, to partner with their *Daddy* as agents of life for the upbuilding of His spiritual kingdom. Created in our Father's image – His Imago Dei, God being a *Divine Spirit Person* (El or Elohim); even so, mankind are spirit-beings (elohim) like their *Daddy*. But are *clothed in flesh*, purposed for and created for eternity, however, without deity, unlike our *Daddy – El,* God eternally existing, as

Three in One – the Triune God (Matthew 3:16,17; Matt. 28:19; 2 Corinthians 13:14). Jesus clothed himself in flesh so that He may provide for fallen humanity a picture of heaven. Man has been clothed in flesh and *Renewed* by the Holy Spirit to represent or be a picture of heaven on earth. How are you doing with this?

The Matters of Theodicy and Free Will

As seen, Yahweh gave birth to *Man,* even so to Israel, His *son* or chosen people… He cared for them… He clothed them… He instructed them… He provided for them… He watched over them… He protected them… He made a way for them… He provided a home for them… He loved them because they were His own! He was their *Loving Daddy and their Difference Maker!* If only *Man* – Adam and Eve and their offspring had remained one or spiritually united with their *Daddy,* they would be blessed for eternity. Nevertheless, our Dad had a foreordained plan. Through Jesus, humanity would be cared for by our *Daddy* as we follow His eternal plan while temporally sojourning on earth.

Provided for us in Genesis Chapter One, all earthly things seen and unseen, God created to meet the needs and satisfy the pleasures of *Man*… and such things were deemed by Him as **good**. Genesis Chapter 1: Foregoing verses 1 to 24… verse 25 reads, *God made the wild animals according to their kinds, the livestock according to their kinds, and all the creatures that move along the ground according to their kinds. And God saw that it was **good**. 26 Then God said, "Let us make mankind in our image, in our likeness, so that they may rule over the fish in the sea and the birds in the sky, over the livestock and all the wild animals, and over all the creatures that move along the ground."*

27 So God created mankind in his own image, in the image of God, he created them; male and female, he created them. 28 God blessed them and said to them, "Be fruitful and increase in number; fill the earth and subdue it. Rule over the fish in the sea and the birds in the sky and over every living creature that moves on the ground."

31 God saw all that he had made, and it was **very good***. And there was evening, and there was morning—the sixth day.* [The NIV version of the Bible will be utilized throughout this book unless indicated otherwise.]

In this portion of Scripture, we see that the text concluded God's creative activity with the statement, *"And God saw that it was* **good.***"* Five other times in the verses preceding verse *twenty-five,* God also said His completed work *was* **good***.* However, it was only after the male and female *Adam* were created that God said His creation was now **very good** – complete or perfect! All that Adam and Eve could embrace with their senses, as well the undiscernible, our loving and caring *Daddy* had created and provided for them, His children, and family who were to represent Him on earth.

However, Adam and Eve's love for and committed relationship with their *Daddy* would be put to the test. Would they remain faithful to their Father... we already know the answer. That which was to test and ultimately tempt them, this tempting being from the evil one, was permitted by God that His prearranged plan of *Man's* redemption may be set in motion (Genesis 3:15 – *the Protoevangelium;* Ephesians 1:4,5; 1 Peter 1:19,20).

Our *Daddy* knows the Devil's every tactic; even so, there are times that He, our loving Father, allows evil to come our way; in this, God's *permissive will* is seen at work... read the Book of Job, but for now, only chapters one and two. In the Book of Job, we are to consider the matter of *Theodicy*. Therein, one encounters the tension and grapples with the Omnipotence, Love, Sovereignty, and Goodness of our *Daddy* in the face of the existence of evil and suffering in this world – hence, Theodicy.

When we consider the inherent evil of *Man*, we must also consider the fact that we are created as *Free-Will* individuals who can choose to commit evil… as with Adam and Eve. Within this study of Theodicy, there is also *Soul-Making*, where suffering and evil serve as tools to develop human virtue and character, making us better and more spiritually mature children of God. Then there is evil and suffering for the *Greater Good* of God's plan and/or our benefit that otherwise could not have been achieved.

In the Scripture, as mentioned above shared from Genesis Chapter 1, *Sin* in the person of this antagonist, Satan – that is, *Sin* personified. This looming and threatening Dilemma – Satan had not yet trespassed and overtaken Adam's garden home, thereby creating a dilemma for Adam, his home, and his offspring perpetually. God had, in fact, established His kingdom here *on Earth as it is in heaven.* Death and corruption were alien to Earth and its new inhabitants. The man and husband, who God *calls* Adam, and His wife, who Adam calls or *names* Eve, her name in Hebrew is *Chavvah – the life giver* or mother of mankind had been purposed and positioned to partner with their Creator… What a privileged, honor!

These two, before their sinful rebellion and resulting alliance with Satan, wanted for nothing. They had their *Daddy*, and He had them… together they were one – a perfect family! God was their *Dad – their Difference Maker*, a great team and family, were they purposed to become. Ultimately and in due time, the children of God will be permanently restored before their *Daddy*! Needless to say, Adam and Eve had everything they needed to have a God-honoring home and to be a victorious couple until that Dilemma – the Devil showed up at Adam's door. Whenever and wherever evil shows up, it always presents a dilemma that must be halted at the door! Or else, the *Dilemma* – hence evil will have its way with you and all that is dear and meaningful to you and our *Daddy!*

The creation of *Man* and God communing with them as their *Dad* in their garden home and mountain paradise, and even their sacred space, was motivated by the Father's love! God wanted to extend His family upon the earth... He wanted children who would see and love Him as their God and Creator but also, lovingly or intimately, call and rely on Him as their *Daddy, the Ultimate Difference Maker* (Romans 8:15)!

How sweet the sound of this term of endearment – Daddy! And what comfort that term brings and what assurance is provided to the child (no matter their age) who has a Daddy to call on and to lean on! Sadly, many children grow up and mature into adults not knowing the comfort and assurance that a Daddy has been purposed to bring.

Too many children are growing up... and this is disastrous and potentially a catastrophic dilemma, not having a dad functioning in their God-giving role and purpose, and equally problematic if not more consequential when one does not know who their Daddy is! When we consider this matter closely, is there any wonder why many find it hard to comprehend God as a loving Father or Dad? Have you found it somewhat odd or difficult to refer to God as your Daddy? Well, you shouldn't... It's His desire for you to see and call on Him as your loving *Daddy!*

This Daddy Dilemma – not having a dad active in my life during my adolescent years and beyond was my reality, an all-too-common troubling theme for many. Interestingly, nearly five decades into my life and while editing my companion book to this volume and a year or so before publishing it. My Daddy Dilemma – this sad, unfortunate, and disadvantageous situation I lived through, I unexpectedly was presented with a surprising, nevertheless, all too common dilemma. A situation thereby causing for a revision to my genealogical history from what I had known. The exact time and date of what would become my revised, revelatory-expanded history was brought to light on the afternoon of Wednesday, April 7th, 2022.

Like many fatherless sons and daughters, years before this new revelation, I, too, as a man and dad in my mid-thirties, longed for the comfort and assurance that only a Daddy can bring. This I also shared in my first book. Later on in this book, I will address this revelation in greater detail and its impact. Yes, I, too, was faced with various dilemmas. However, in God, my Creator, while I was a young man, He showed up in my life and became my *Dad, the Ultimate Difference Maker!*

From Very Good - To What Happened And What's Next?

You see, what happened was… God, who is Love, had created *Man* with volition or free will to express themselves. God's creative process after forming *Man* was complete and perfect – hence, "very good!" However, as already seen, Adam and Eve chose to rebel against their *Spiritual Dad* instead of reciprocally loving and honoring Him in return. I will not address the various ideas or conjectures of love or counter this world's notion of love as I did in my previous book.

However, what I will say is this, love is not merely a feeling or secondhand emotion. It is who our *Daddy* is, an attribute of His essence that helplessly causes Him to care for you and me immeasurably, no matter how messed up we are! This Love, or God Himself, His essence He longs to impart, or spiritually birth within His children, thereby enabling the child of God to conform to His standard of righteousness in and through love as we commune together.

Our *Daddy's* love for us is like the love of an earthly parent that causes them to express to their child[ren], "I love you to the moon and Back!" Or a dad, spreading his arms apart as wide as he can while saying, "I love you this much!" Or him saying, "My love for you is wider than the widest ocean and deeper than the deepest seas!" These expressions of love are communicated in simple terms yet profoundly sending a message to the child who hears these words and sees the demonstration of a parent's love for them. It's a love that a parent has for their offspring that knows no end, no matter the age of their offspring or the wrong they may do.

This should go without saying, but there is a need: a dad should also be able to assure their child of their love for them by simply saying, "I love you because you are mine, and then faithfully demonstrate their love! This very sentiment is how God, our eternally existing *Spiritual Daddy,* feels about us! He loves us because we are His… Period! We are, in fact, created in His image or *Tselem.* This Hebrew rendering means our external demonstration or mirroring of our *Father* as intellectual, creative, rational, and relational individuals – His physical imagers as earth dwellers (Genesis 1:26,27).

And in "His likeness," – *Demut,* a Hebrew word, denoting our eternal and internal essence or likeness as we are to possess the righteousness, caring, and loving nature of our *Daddy*. Now underscoring, we are begotten or created by our Father. Henceforth, as *eternal spirits* to live out or display our *Daddy's* nature for all to experience. Humanity has been clothed in flesh – our outer covering that our Daddy has chosen to dress us with (1 Corinthians 15: 39-41).

Even so, our bodily temples, as they pertain to the children of God who are indwelt by the Holy Spirit. That we may rightly represent our Father as His imagers – *Tselem,* here on earth (1 Corinthians 6:19,20). In Hebrew, the word for flesh is *basar,* and in Greek, it's *sarx.* These renderings of flesh primarily provide, but not exclusively, an understanding of our temporary terrestrial composition due to sin until we are provided by our *Daddy* with our incorruptible and new bodies or physical attire.

That said, our *Daddy's* love does not waver or diminish when He is disappointed with us when we rebel against His will in thought or our actions through our flesh. Nevertheless, Scripture is clear, our *Daddy* disciplines those who belong to Him. This should also be the case with earthly parents or God's caretakers, whereby administering discipline or corrective action to their and God's little ones when it's needed and until they reach the age of personal accountability. After which, as Christians, we are to seek counsel or correction through the Word of God and by other Believers in Christ – His Church.

Listen to these words according to Hebrews 12: 5: *And have you completely forgotten this word of encouragement that addresses you as a father addresses his son? It says, "My son, do not make light of the Lord's discipline, and do not lose heart when he rebukes you, 6 because the Lord disciplines the one he loves, and he chastens everyone he accepts as his son." 7 Endure hardship as discipline; God is treating you as his children. For what children are not disciplined by their father?*

*8 If you are not disciplined—and everyone undergoes discipline—then you are not legitimate, not true sons and daughters at all. 9 Moreover, we have all had human fathers who disciplined us, and we respected them for it. How much more should we submit to the **Father of spirits** and live! 10 They disciplined us for a little while as they thought best; but God disciplines us for our good, in order that we may share in his holiness. 11 No discipline seems pleasant at the time, but painful. Later on, however, it produces a harvest of righteousness and peace for those who have been trained by it.*

Additionally:

1. **Proverbs 13:24** (ESV):
"Whoever spares the rod hates his son, but he who loves him is diligent to discipline him."

2. **Proverbs 22:15** (ESV):
"Folly is bound up in the heart of a child, but the rod of discipline drives it far from him."

3. **Proverbs 23:13-14** (ESV):
"Do not withhold discipline from a child; if you strike him with a rod, he will not die. If you strike him with the rod, you will save his soul from Sheol."

4. **Proverbs 29:15** (ESV):
"The rod and reproof give wisdom, but a child left to himself brings shame to his mother."

Furthering my thoughts on the matter of love. Love can only be expressed through one *freely* extending it to some other through their words followed by their actions. Or one's actions followed by their words, the two expressions are bound together. However, it's one's actions in expressing love that can speak far louder and more profoundly than one's words. For the individual having experienced love in action from a loved one, then one's expression of the words I love you becomes more meaningful!

Perhaps you've heard someone say, "I love you so much; if I could, I would give you the world!" Well, this is precisely what our *Daddy* did for mankind. He gave us the world! However, Adam and Eve, our foreparents, did not appreciate what their Father had provided for them and gifted them with. Consequently, the world was then led into chaos resulting from their ingratitude and disobedience!

But because of the love of our *Daddy*, He could not give up on His children! If the world given to *Man* wasn't enough for the children of His making to see just how much He adored and cared for them. ***Then He would display His love through the Best Gift ever... He would sacrificially give of Himself, even so, His Existent Son – Jesus, Love personified*** (Romans 5:8; John 15:13; 1 John 4:9,10)! Jesus, in obedience to His Father, furthermore, eternally possessing the mind of His *Abba or Daddy* because He is "One" with or "equal to His Father," would humble Himself and take on the form of *Man.* Yet, without partaking of humanity's corruption in the flesh or *Man's* sinful nature (Philippians 2:5-8; John 10:30; John 14:9,10).

Jesus would experience our pain and suffering and willingly take upon Himself our just or due punishment for sin because of His love for us! He would, as *The Ultimate Difference Maker,* confront and deal with this world's or our personal antagonist, this bully – *Death* or *Satan!* Jesus would overcome this nemesis and grievous, oppressive, and pestering maleficent spirit-being who is behind all that is evil. Jesus did this out of love for us, in order that His *Daddy's* wayward children may be freed from the penalty of their sins, its consequences, and the fear of *Death* – even so, Satan himself, this world's ultimate Dilemma (1 Corinthians 15:50-57; Hebrews 2:14,15; Revelation 1:17,18)!

As seen in the life of Jesus, this is the kind of difference a Daddy is supposed to make: To rid his child[ren] of all fears, as he imparts life lessons to his offspring. And, more importantly, while pointing them to *The Life-giver,* their *Creator, Protector,* and even their Heavenly Father. As a godly dad, and having measured up to his responsibilities. In his continued ministry as priest over his home he is to pray for the salvation of his children that is offered through the sacrifice and love of God's *Distinct Son – Jesus!*

The ones to whom God's personified *Love* – Jesus is extended and embraced are such individuals who have freely received this Love granted to them. Or, one has the prerogative or free will to be unaccepting or nonreciprocal and even unappreciative of this *Gift of Love* when presented. These expressions – accepting or rejecting Jesus are generally or are readily noticeable. Nevertheless, where love is extended and is seemingly accepted and reciprocated, it is only through testing, or when an individual's love is tried, that one is able to determine if love is true, genuine, and/or faithful from the recipient of God's Love.

This testing of one's love cannot come about apart from the exercise of free will. *Free will* is an aspect of humanity that is also after the likeness of our Creator or *Daddy.* It is that part of us and the expression of free will that brings a family or people together in love. Or the outworking of one's free will that can irreversibly divide, rip apart, and destroy families and relationships, making individuals and groups of people hated enemies because of lovelessness. Or because of lovelessness, a people or person viewed as less-than and/or a mere commodity and even an inconvenience.

If God is Love and He is, which is to be expressed in and through relationships. Where, then, is the origin of hate and division… But from none other than the Devil himself! Whose sole purpose is to pervert, if not destroy, any resemblance of God's character that is to be exercised or manifested through *Man* and the relationships we forge, in particular, the relationship of marriage and the family that is built through this loving and lovely union of *man with woman as ordained of God.*

Our *Daddy* wanted to enlarge and extend His family from heaven to earth, and therefore, He created *Man.* This family or relationally intimate and loving bond that God desires for mankind cannot happen or be maintained without Him. When Adam and Eve were perfectly aligned because they were in line or allied with their *Dad,* He responded that creation was in a *very good* place… all was well in the home that God established! However, the test of their love and faithfulness toward their *Dad* and even one another would be put to the test.

As for What Happened… Adam and Eve's Failure during Testing

In Genesis Chapter 2, Scripture gives us the following account:

8 Now the Lord God had planted a garden in the east, in Eden; and there he put the man he had formed. 9 The Lord God made all kinds of trees grow out of the ground—trees that were pleasing to the eye and good for food. In the middle of the garden were the Tree of Life and the Tree of the Knowledge of Good and Evil.

A few verses following:

15 The Lord God took the man and put him in the Garden of Eden to work it and take care of it. 16 And the Lord God **commanded the man**, *"You are free to eat from any tree in the garden; 17 but you must not eat from the tree of the knowledge of good and evil, for when you eat from it,* **you will certainly die.**" Hence, to be separated from God, the Source of Eternal Life - *Zoe*!

Death – this dread by many means for *Man* (like a plant removed from soil) to be *spiritually* separated, removed from, and devoid of God our *Daddy*, who is *Eternal Life* and the *Giver and Sustainer of Life*. Indeed, every creature in heaven and under heaven is sustained or is kept and given life by God (John 15:1-5; Colossians 1:21-23). This matter and manner of death – detachment spiritually from our Creator, *Dad*, even so, separation from the Holy Spirit is what we incurred or inherited through Adam. Thus, upon our physical birth into this fallen or sinful world, we are, in fact, dead in our sin, in need of spiritually being *Born Again* – brought back to the love and family of *God the Father* by the *Living Word of God* and sustained by the power of *God the Indwelling Holy Spirit* (John Chapter 3).

Furthermore, it is to be understood that our spiritual reality can only be truly conceptualized with the help of the Holy Spirit. Likewise, that we are born into this world spiritually dead because of the Edenic Fall is *Man's* reality that is clearly brought to light, and all this entails by God the Spirit (1 Corinthians 2:14; John 16:13; Romans 8:5-7). The fall of *Man* climaxed and culminated with mankind's physical death and all the evil mankind has hellishly unleashed directly and otherwise upon his fellowman – his brothers and sisters and sons and daughters. *Man's* actions – humanity's rage and terror, and our choices have led to the immeasurable suffering that those living in this fallen world have been subjected to (Romans 5:12; Genesis 2:17).

When Adam ate from the forbidden tree, spiritual separation from God is that which He and Eve experienced immediately. Their offspring – humanity, you and I, at conception, therefore, have inherited their sin-nature and are, consequently, also separated from God. Hopefully, you can now grasp the urgent necessity that a child born of a woman must be raised to know God for themselves, that they need to be reborn spiritually of God and reconnected by the indwelling Holy Spirit back to their loving God and our *Daddy* is of dire importance! I remind you, Satan is after our children! I will argue unwaveringly, more so today than ever before!

In Genesis Chapter 3, the unfolding and climatic beginning of the end, of that which was ***very good*** – that is, *Man's* defection and rejection of their *Daddy's* love and their subsequent expulsion from the Garden of Eden is provided for us here in the following text:

1 Now the serpent was more crafty than any of the wild animals the Lord God had made. He said to the woman, "Did God really say, 'You must not eat from any tree in the garden'?"2 The woman said to the serpent, "We may eat fruit from the trees in the garden, 3 but God did say, 'You must not eat fruit from the tree that is in the middle of the garden, and you must not touch it, or you will die.'"4"You will not certainly die," the serpent said to the woman. 5"For God knows that when you eat from it, your eyes will be opened, and you will be like God, knowing good and evil."

6 When the woman saw that the fruit of the tree was good for food and pleasing to the eye and also desirable for gaining wisdom, she took some and ate it. She also gave some to her husband, who was with her, and he ate it. 7 Then the eyes of both of them were opened, and they realized they were naked; so they sewed fig leaves together and made coverings for themselves. 8 Then the man and his wife heard the sound of the Lord God as he was walking in the garden in the cool of the day, and they hid from the Lord God among the trees of the garden.

9 But the Lord God called to the man (specifically, not Eve), "Where are you?"

*10 **He** answered, "I heard you in the garden, and I was afraid because I was naked, so I hid."*

11 And he said, "Who told you that you were naked? Have you eaten from the tree that I commanded you not to eat from?"

*12 The **man said**, "The woman you put here with me—she gave me some fruit from the tree, and I ate it."*

13 Then the Lord God said to the woman, "What is this you have done?"

The woman said, "The serpent deceived me, and I ate."

14 So the Lord God said to the serpent, "Because you have done this, "Cursed are you above all livestock and all wild animals! You will crawl on your belly, and you will eat dust all the days of your life. 15 And I will put enmity between you and the woman, and between your offspring (seed KGV) and hers; he will crush your head, and you will strike his heel." 16 To the woman, he said, "I will make your pains in childbearing very severe; with painful labor, you will give birth to children. Your desire will be for your husband, and he will rule over you."

*17 To Adam, he said, "Because **you listened to your wife** and ate fruit from the tree about which I commanded you, 'You must not eat from it,'"Cursed is* *the ground because of you; through painful toil, you will eat food from it all the days of your life. 18 It will produce thorns and thistles for you, and you will eat the plants of the field. 19 By the sweat of your brow, you will eat your food until you return to the ground, since from it you were taken; for dust you are and to dust you will return."*

*20 Adam **named his wife Eve** because she would become the mother of all the living.*

*21 The Lord God made garments of skin for Adam and his wife and clothed them. 22 And the Lord God said, "**The man** has now become like one of us, knowing good and evil. **He** must not be allowed to reach out his hand and take also from the tree of life and eat and live forever." 23 So the Lord God banished **him** from the Garden of Eden to work the ground from which **he** had been taken. 24 After he drove the **man** out, he placed on the east side of the Garden of Eden cherubim and a flaming sword flashing back and forth to guard the way to the tree of life.*

Notice from the emboldened words:

God initially calls out Adam. Why? He was created first; humanity originated from him. Adam was God's designated leader or Federal Head of God's kingdom or earthly domain. He was given the command to leave the forbidden tree alone! It was he who named the animals as well as his wife, Eve. Therefore, God called out to Adam, His appointed leader, "Where are you?"... I hold you responsible for this colossal failure. Because of the *Law of first mention*, as has been presented. I will further argue that God has also appointed men to pastor or be leaders over his house – the Church, and not women, not even as co-pastors (Matthew 21:13; Hebrews 3:6; 1 Timothy 3:1-7; Titus 1:5-9).

Returning to the Genesis narrative:

From this reading, now, you can plainly see what happened to that which God had deemed to be *very good. Man* was disloyal, unfaithful, and showed indifference in response to their *Daddy's* love. They failed the test of loyalty and loving commitment in their familial relationship with God, their *Daddy,* and with one another. Subsequently, they began finger-pointing instead of acknowledging their wrong and infidelity.

Countless pages can be written, and a multitude of life lessons can be gleaned from within the few Scriptures provided on the life of Adam and Eve. A major dilemma and countless dilemmas *Man* would now be faced with because they chose to be disobedient to their *Daddy.* As for the principal or most significant and consequential dilemma, Adam and Eve's or *Man's* separation from God – hence death, both spiritual and physical! And secondly, the Devil's attack upon Adam's home and his failure to defend it, whereby giving it and his wife over to the Devil.

But not just his home did Adam, without a fight, give to the Devil; he also lost the dominion rule that was bestowed upon him by his *Dad* over the earth as *God's Man-king* and appointed head over his castle or home. God wants faithful Man-kings as leaders over the homes that are established under His loving and protecting rule. On the other hand, and adversarially, self-appointed *Women-kings* and those females of like-mind, I deem, are women who are refusing to submit to Jesus' authority and make Him their Lord over their lives.

In need of spiritual renewal or, as a child of God, a transformation from carnal or worldly thinking, they are therefore incapable or unwilling to submit and be led by a godly husband. Or, as presented, a Man-king of God's making and positioning. As for women holding positions of authority in the Church, nowhere does Scripture ascribe a Church's leadership title to women. Although there were influential women in the Bible who were used by God as Difference Makers, God has appointed men to lead both of His houses – our individual homes and the Church universally. Make no mistake about it, a Woman-king is not after God's design and purpose; however, a submitted and God-honoring Queen… Yes!. Therefore, a Woman-king, this fictional or perverted character of Satan's or society's making, should remain on television, on the movie screen, or in fictional books. And not in God's house!

As for a godly woman or a Queen who knows how to reign under subjection to God and in submission to her Man-king's leading, such a man – one who has subjected himself to their Daddy's authority – becomes the leader God has purposefully designed him to be. This ensures that there may be order and accountability in their homes, which are an extension of our Father's kingdom. The man follows God's lead, and in turn, the woman follows her husband's lead, who follows God's lead. This home governance is patterned after God's ordering in heaven (1 Corinthians 11:3; Ephesians 5:21-33; Colossians 3:18,19; 1 Peter 3:1-7; Daniel 7:9-10; Revelation 4:2-11).

Now, don't mistake my Scriptural understanding by thinking that I am diminishing the strength and worth of God's gift – the woman to her husband. Far from it! God's daughters and His sons are ontological equals, as I've previously elucidated. One is not better than the other, and neither is our *Daddy's* love preferential. However, biologically, we have been given functions and roles and even rules by which we are to live under and be subject to or governed as our Daddy's royal children who have been permitted to unite with Him and one day live in our Father's kingdom forever.

Resulting from Adam's failure to show up and to present himself forcefully and fearless before the Devil as a Mighty man of God – God's Difference Maker – Adam lost not only his perfect relationship with God but also his perfect wife! In this failure, Adam transitioned from being God's Difference Maker to becoming a catastrophic global dilemma. Additionally, Adam lost Eve in this sense, the unity and mutual respect they were to share within a God-centered or God-governed and ordered home (Genesis 3:16; Gen.4:7).

In the Scriptures provided, the word "desire" – *teshuqah* in Hebrew can be understood as taking control or being in control over someone. Because of the fall, Eve's of the world would now desire to wear the pants. While Adam's of the world would misuse their authority.

The woman, Eve, who through design was by extension of their Creator, *bone of Adam's bone*, a female addition and version of himself and a *gift* from God. However, because Adam failed to **correct** his wife in love, even so, himself, his female representative, and to **protect** her, yet again even himself with the truth or prohibition of God's word, there would now be trouble in paradise and various challenges perpetually with maintaining godly homes and marriages (Gen. 2:24; Matthew 19:5; Mark 10:8).

I say again: One of the major challenges or dilemmas facing marriages due to Adam's failure would be some husband's misuse or abuse of authority. And some wives who are unwilling or who struggle to submit to their husbands as head of a God-ordained home.

Unwilling to address the threat that showed up at his door, Adam, through his passive presence, allowed his wife to be violated and manipulated by the Devil! And consequently, their unity and the home that God established to be divided. Adam was complicit as he seemingly unashamedly looked on and did not act! He failed to step in and step up as the shepherd and protector of his wife and their sacred space. Adam failed to sacrificially love his wife! Even so, through his inaction and the love that was to be put into action, he showed a lack of love or care that he had for himself. Adam became a dilemma! In his inaction and failure to show up and function in his purposed role, families and marriages until this world's end would face disastrous dilemmas and challenges of various sorts (1 Corinthians 11:3; Ephesians 5: 22-31; Eph. 4:14,15. Additionally read Romans 5:12-19; 1 Corinthians 15:21,22).

My brothers, what I am about to say to you, and in particular those of you who are Dads, may be hard to receive by some... but prayerfully hear me out. We are engaged in brutal spiritual warfare (Ephesians 6:10-20; 1 Peter 5:8)! When the Serpent showed up at the doorstep of Adam, he didn't extend an Olive Branch to him, nor did the Devil bring him a Peace Offering... No! He showed up deceptively as *Death* to declare spiritual war against Adam's territory, to disrupt God's house and plan for humanity! With Eve locked in his sights, this adversary – Satan lusted after her so that he may overcome Adam's and *Man's* purpose and familial position of unity in oneness with God, their *Daddy*!

And so, here it is, my brothers: A man or dad who is present in his house and yet fails to come under God's authority... I will emphasize my point, who fails to yield and align himself and those under his care with God our Creator and *Daddy's authority*. Such a Dad, in all the "good" you may do and the 'love' you may express toward your family. Apart from God, it's *dead works* that you are carrying out that don't satisfy the souls or spiritual longings of your family. Such works or actions on your part that do not impart spiritual life nor point or lead your household to their *Daddy our Eternal Life-Giver* is useless and done in vain, when all is said and done

(Luke 9:25; Ecclesiastes 2:11; Eccl. 12:13,14)! Until we are aligned and allied with our Creator, we are indeed disoriented men - Dilemmas who are in need of His reorientation!

Yes, you may be a good provider and great protector and are accountable to your family. Still, and more importantly, or weightier, you have not made yourself answerable to God. Therefore, if there is no change in your position or orientation with God and in how you lead your family. I'm sorry to say this, but in the end, and in the sight of your Creator, you are no better than a man who has neglected the care of his child[ren] or who has walked out on his wife and kids. Or that man who has never acknowledged his own offspring and paternal responsibility.

Such a man Satan has him where he wants him and where he desires to keep him and his family – away from God. That is, having been deceived that your good works are good enough, you have kept those under your care from lining up and aligning your home with our Heavenly Father – *The Ultimate Difference Maker!* I present to you what the Scriptures say regarding being apart from God, *that we are spiritually dead because of sin; even so, you are one with the Devil, your father* (Colossians 2:13; John 8:44).

Such a man who neglects or fails his family in this regard is, in fact, Dad – The Dilemma! Death, although this may not appear to be the case by mankind's or this world's standard or measure of success. Nevertheless, the dominion of the Devil you and your family are under. Subsequently, you have failed your family, you as a Dad having neglected to lead your family to Life – God Himself… I say again, apart from Him, we are all dead before our Creator! (Ephesians 2:1,2; Colossians 2:13; Matthew 16:26; Matt. 4:4). As it was for Adam, before God, we are held accountable; to Him we will have to answer!

The lifeless family dynamics I've presented. They being dead, absent from a familial relationship with God, can be layered, varying in complications, and surely consequential and negatively affecting families or individuals for generations! This generational dilemma and its effects can be referred to as spiritual strongholds or generational curses and bondage, which need to be halted and reversed by godly men who have been purposed by God to be their family's first line of defense as Difference Makers. This spiritual matter or spiritual warfare has been laid out before you. Are you... or have you decided to become a Dad, the Difference Maker, or are you... and will you remain a *Dad, the Dilemma*?

These dilemmas or negative consequences due to spiritual brokenness and conflict, which show their ugly heads in a variety of ways, are also made apparent in the lovelessness of people towards other people, in one's lack of empathy, dislike, or abhorrence towards one of God's offspring. We all, saved or sinner, Jew or Gentile, with melanin in our skin or not, belong to God. We are His people. Our Creator or *Daddy's* love is towards us all equally!

Needless to say, what is more than evident in this fallen and corrupt world are the various degrees of brokenness or sin-sickness that have overtaken mankind and are made ever so apparent in the numerous fatherless and dysfunctional homes... what a dilemma we are faced with! Only when men are raised up under or restored to their *Daddy* as *kings* and *Mighty men of God* will we begin to see a change for the better. However, not likely exponential changes in this fallen world that belong to the Devil. But at least a better outcome and end result for you and your house that has been united with our *Daddy* through Jesus (John Chapter 14; John. 10:14-18)!

What's Next?
A Closer Look at the Spiritual Realm: their Intent and God's Response to Their Rebellion

As for *"What's Next?"* Having mentioned, in general, man's historical dilemmas because of sin or the Edenic Fall – the first earthly rebellion. We must return our attention to the aforementioned Scripture in Genesis Chapter 3. However, not limited to this content for God's answer to what was next regarding addressing *Man's* dilemmas, with the most consequential dilemma occurring when Adam intentionally or willfully rebelled against his Creator in contrast to Eve, who was deceived and, therefore, partook from the forbidden tree (Gen. 3:1-6 & 13; 1 Timothy 2:14).

Let me first remind you why the Devil harbors such disdain for both you and me. His enmity arises not only from his pride but from a deep resentment toward God, his Maker. Additionally, because of the hatred against his Creator, whom he was and is incapable of warring against, his fury and madness drive him to target God's creation – mankind. Unable to challenge God directly, the Devil's malice is turned toward us, those created in God's image. This is why, from the very beginning, he attacked Adam, seeking to corrupt what God had made perfect in an attempt to thwart God's plan of establishing His family and kingdom on earth.

The Devil's attacks continue relentlessly against humanity, aided by the rebellious heavenly host – fallen angels who followed him in his defiance. He despises the godly potential that resides in each of us, knowing that God has woven a divine purpose into our lives, both individually and within families. This potential, enabled and empowered by God, is a constant reminder of the destiny the Devil forfeited through his rebellion. Amongst other things, he loathes the possibility of us walking in the fullness of God's plan, which reflects God's goodness and power. Through God's guidance, families can thrive, bringing glory to their Creator, whom we intimately call *Daddy*. This intimacy with God, both as individuals and in the context of our families, is what the Devil seeks to destroy, knowing that it reflects the very relationship he lost in his fall from grace.

The Devil, or specifically Satan, formerly known as Lucifer, meaning "Light-bringer" or "Morning Star." But there was a change in his designation and position resulting from his change in disposition and self-imposed purpose to rebel against his Creator. This fallen high-ranking angel or cherub, who also had become a prideful megalomaniac, lusted to be like God. Likewise, he coveted praise that was due to God alone! He was not satisfied with his God's designed **position** and **function.** A ministry granted to him by His Creator as one privileged and **purposed** to praise and worship God in the service of His Creator's kingdom.

Furthermore, others from God's heavenly family, these heavenly hosts, or fallen angelic beings (elohim), followed Lucifer in his rebellion. Lucifer wanted adulation; such honor and reverence was to be bestowed upon our Creator and unto Him alone! Lucifer, having rebelled against God his Creator, lost his standing before his *Maker* and was subsequently expelled or disqualified from his heavenly abode, his family, and the relationship that he once lovingly shared with his Creator. Consequently, and justly, he has been eternally condemned for his act of treason (Isaiah 14:12-15; Ezekiel 28:12-19; Revelation 12:7-9). There must be order in God's house! Likewise, there will be consequences for those who remain in rebellion!

Let's take a look at the fallout and God's judgment against Satan. Genesis Chapter 3 reads: *14 So the Lord God said to the serpent, "Because you have* *done this, "Cursed are you above all livestock and all wild animals! You will crawl on your belly, and you will eat dust all the days of Your life. 15 And I will put enmity between you and the woman, and between your **offspring** (seed KGV) and hers; **it** (He) will crush your head, and you will strike **his** heel"[NIV].*

Drawing your attention to verse 15, God said to the serpent, aka the Devil. *"I will put enmity between **you** and the **woman**. And between your **offspring** (seed KGV) and hers, **He** will crush your head, and you will **strike his heel**."* Listen carefully to what was just said regarding the ***seed of a woman***. This is an unusual expression or Old Testament mystery that I will bring clarity to as you further your reading in this section, with greater understanding coming in Chapter 2 of this book.

I have pointed out that Lucifer declared war against God, his very Creator, with his cosmic rebellion in an attempt to elevate himself to be like God. Expelled from the kingdom of God, He then set his fiendish gaze on *Man*, the apple of God's eye, as his target or objective for utter destruction! I personally have experienced a notable first-hand attack from the satanic realm, as detailed in my first book. This evil realm of spiritual darkness is astutely aware that it cannot stand against God and that their days are numbered. Therefore, this realm of spiritual wickedness is seeking with urgent vengefulness to either destroy mankind or so pervert one's God-designed function and purpose that they, too, are disqualified from God's eternal kingdom.

Before his fall, the Devil was in perfect familial harmony with his Creator. Likewise, mankind was created to be in a perfect relationship with God, and we are reborn to belong to the royal family of our heavenly Father. While we inhabit this terrestrial realm, those in the celestial realm have in common with us, volition. However, free will comes with negative consequences, particularly when we choose to act outside the will of our Creator. This point is underscored by the verses from Genesis chapter 3, which illustrate the repercussions of disobedience.

Due to the Devil's deliberate betrayal and defiance against his Creator, he has been condemned to the Gehenna, the place of eternal suffering (Revelation 19:20; Revelation 20:10-15; Daniel 7:11). This place of torment was initially purposed or allotted to him and other willfully disobedient rebel angels (elohim), referred to as fallen angels. The following angelic titles, as provided throughout Scripture, demonstrate God's hierarchy and order within Heaven or the celestial realm:

The Sovereign God or Triune God!

Followed perhaps by this ordering:

1. The Sons of God – Job 1:6 & 2:1 or Divine Council – Psalm 82:1,6.
2. Archangels (Michael) – Jude 1:9.
3. Seraphim – Isaiah 6:2.
4. Cherubim – Ezekiel 10:1,2.
5. Lesser angels (Gabriel) – Daniel 8:16; Luke 1:19; Hebrews 1:14.

And lastly, the rebellious angels which are also ranked (Ephesians 6:12; Daniel 10:13,20; Colossians 1:16).

This heavenly ordering serves as a picture of what is to be mirrored within our earthly or terrestrial realm. However, all who reject Jesus have aligned themselves with Satan's kingdom. Those who decline Jesus' invitation to Salvation will, therefore, be joined to Satan's cohorts and his kingdom of evil in the *Lake of Fire* – the Gehenna (Hell) from both realms. This has been Satan's plan from the beginning – if he is going down, he intends to take as many as he can with him.

These former representatives of God's heavenly host abandoned their first assignments, marking the first of two rebellions among the heavenly beings. Genesis 6 narrates a distinct and second rebellion of the elohim, or fallen angels, who also left their first estate as well. These rebellious "sons of God," referenced in Genesis 6, were and are, therefore, presently confined to the prison of Hades, which is also broadly known as Sheol. Sheol (Hebrew) and Hades (Greek) both refer to the realm of the dead, where the righteous await their resurrected bodies and the wicked anticipate their ultimate judgment. However, within Sheol (or Hades), there is also Tartarus – the specific, permanent holding place of torment for the fallen elohim who rebelled in Genesis 6.

Then, there is the Abyss (or Bottomless Pit), a temporary imprisonment referenced in the New Testament specifically for wicked or unclean spirits – demons of a different order. These elohim, currently confined in the Abyss, will be released, as described in Revelation 9:1-11. For more clarity regarding these elohim, read the following scriptures: Genesis 6:1-7, Job 38:4-7, Matthew 25:41, 2 Peter 2:4, and Jude 1:6.

Unlike mankind, who was and is tempted and deceived into rebellion, these elohim will not have a redemption song to sing, as referenced in Revelation 14:3. Instead, they will wail in perpetual torment, forever excluded from God's presence and family. People of God's making, my brothers and sisters, and fellow imagers of our Creator and/or *Dad*, this total exclusion or separation from God and His grace embodies the essence of their torment – dead apart from God. As disembodied spirit beings, while in this eternal state, they will experience suffering without end!

I must emphasize. This eternal prison of immense suffering within the Gehenna will also house **all** who defy and reject the Love of their *Daddy* – Jesus Himself – *Love* personified as displayed in the life of the Father's *Unique Son*. And, too, as presented upon the cross where Jesus hung and gave His life as a sacrifice for you and me! People of my *Daddy's* creating, this act here was the complete and perfect display of *Love* being tested and Love having conquered all – the grave and, most significantly, the Devil, aka Death, which he personified (John 3:16; John 8:19; John 14:7; John 15:13; 1 John 4:8).

Men, It's Time to Give Our All

Men, I pray that you can comprehend that the love of our *Divine Daddy* is immeasurable! *It's* longsuffering and self-sacrificing that *Life* – that is life eternal may be given to all under His care! And so, Dads, how do you measure up in your love towards those under your care? You were graced by your Creator and *Daddy* to bring forth the gift of life – your offspring. Are you there for them… Are you leading them to their *Daddy – The Difference Maker,* the One who gives eternal life?

People of God's making, He wants you to know this truth: the death and eternal suffering of His sinful and rebellious children is not His desire (2 Timothy 2:3,4; 2 Peter 3:9; Ezekiel 18:32). Remember that He loves each of us so much that He gave to this world His very own *Unique Son* that we may be brought back into our *Daddy's* family and His loving care! In so doing, our *Daddy* also suffered with His Son! The *Triune God* accepted and endured this tremendous grief and suffering because they wanted to restore our sinful and broken souls to fellowship with our *Daddy!*

Beloved of God, you, the people of His making… this here, the self-sacrifice of Jesus, demonstrates the love of our Triune God (John 10:10; John 14:1-4, 14-18; Revelation 21:1)! Dads, as imagers of God, this is the kind of love that we as godly fathers and husbands are to give – our all and best for those who have been entrusted to our care! Following the example of our heavenly Father. Dads, you should be willing to suffer for your offspring! Not only that, a loving, godly dad and you godly men should also experience the anguish of your souls when there is suffering within your family and those under your care and influence.

Sadly, it is necessary for me to say that a child should never have to suffer because of a delinquent, derelict, and spiritually destitute dad who is or has become a dilemma for his offspring and family! Tragically, we are seeing too much suffering because of this Daddy Dilemma! Therefore, ***Men, It's Time to Give Our All!***

In case you are in need of a reminder: The woman's child, who God said would crush or deliver a fatal blow to the head of the serpent, this child is none other than Jesus! He was and is the answer to *"What's Next?"* The sinless life that He lived, the love that Jesus had for you and me, and the love and loyalty He had for His *Daddy* compelled Him to secure His cross of suffering so that we may have everlasting *Life* as men and Dads, the Difference Makers!

Jesus knew His *Daddy's* love for Him; He knew how love was to respond to the Dilemma – the Devil, our *Adversary*. Jesus had a *Dad* who led by example. Therefore, He lovingly and sacrificially responded to the help of His Father's lost and broken children. Jesus came to give Himself – His all for you and me! Now, we, as imagers of Jesus, must give our all to our offspring and all who have been entrusted to our care, even so, those under our influence!

CHAPTER 2

Disdain For Daddy,
Therefore Hatred of Men

A Reminder of Our Sin Condition:
We are All in Need of Long-term Healthcare

Before I approach what may be for some of you and for different reasons, this profoundly concerning and sensitive matter as presented in the title, *Disdain For Daddy, Therefore Hatred Of Men*. It is of significant importance that we once again recognize and acknowledge that because of *Man's* fall or our sinful conditions and, therefore, wicked inclinations. That each of us, in varying measures, were and are a broken and messed up group of individuals. As for those of us who have God as our *Daddy*, we acknowledge that we are saved and, even so, an ongoing spiritual work in progress, as we are aided by His grace and the indwelling Holy Spirit.

Unfortunately, we don't have to look far to see that some people – *Saved* and unsaved alike are more broken and messed up than others! Now, make sure you look into the mirror as you draw your conclusion as it pertains to those you have determined are broken and messed up. That said, perhaps you, too, praise God our *Daddy* as I do by expressing, "Thank you for who I've become!" Acknowledging in gratitude and praise to and because of *Daddy's* guidance, counsel, and wisdom *that we are not who we used to be!* Nevertheless, my brothers and sisters in Christ, we have not been made perfect; we still live within our corrupt or sin-sick bodies; therefore, and again, in varying measures, we all remain a work in progress.

As for those who are Christians or children of God, we are more readily, or at least we should be, while becoming more spiritually mature, able to identify and acknowledge the mess that we once really were. Even so, acknowledging the challenges or battles that we war against internally and also against such spiritual evil or threats that are from without or of this demonically influenced world.

By taking this opening approach before unpacking my thoughts on the matters to be undertaken in this chapter, I want to make it clear to you, men and women, boys and girls, all who are such broken, messed up, struggling, and hurting people. Know this truth... You are the beloved of our *Daddy* or your Creator no matter who you are, what you've done, or what may have been done to you! This is simply because God loves you... He is your Creator and Redeemer! And therefore, we, our *Daddy's* children specifically, are to be loving as He is loving, showing empathy to all who are struggling with this life's challenges (Matthew 22:36-39; John 13:35; 1 John 4:8).

It was and is because of our fallen condition, our hurting, broken, and pitiful state, that our *Rescuer, Comforter,* and *Healer* – Jesus, while clothing Himself in flesh, came to this dismal and sinfully devastated world to address head-on, our debilitating and often destructive spiritual dilemmas. He came to us as our *Disaster Relief Agent* to render aid to mankind who were and are presently faced with many spiritually devitalizing and disastrous dilemmas, and most importantly, to confront spiritual evil and restore *Man* from being spiritually dead – separated or cut off from their *Daddy*!

We all were, and even now, some more than others, are in need of immediate and intense spiritual-medical care, and all of us, even long-term spiritual health care! And so, are some of you really so cold and callous of heart, so self-centered and self-righteous that you can frown and sneer upon the spiritually sick; turn up your nose on those who are broken, who are ridiculed, and thereby show no remorse or empathy for God's lost and troubled offspring? If you consider yourself a child of God, with this kind of attitude, you must admit that you are not representing your *Daddy* as you should. Or it may mean that you are only a Christian nominally, and therefore, you are not one within my *Daddy's* kingdom (Matthew 25:34-46).

Jesus made it clear that His *Daddy's* children, each of us, was and are in need of *The Great Physician – God our Healer.* Our Father, therefore, came into this world through His exact Imager – Jesus, His *Unique, Preeminent, Existent, and Distinct Son* as our spiritual and emotional *Caregiver. The Healer* of our souls to see about us and meet every need of His *Daddy's* offspring – the people of His Father's making who have been overcome by this great evil – sin-sickness, and/or spiritual death (Luke 5:31; Isaiah 53:5; Hebrews 9:28; 1 Peter 2:24,25)!

The care and health system that Jesus provides from His Father's kingdom is infinitely better than Obamacare or any medical care this world has to offer! The care systems of this world can only treat our physical illnesses but not cure or eradicate them. These care systems may also be able to assist in enhancing our lives physically and emotionally. But it is only Jesus who can give us eternal life, heal us, and eradicate *Death* and all forms of sickness and diseases that ooze and spew from our fleshly corruption, emotional imbalances, and/or even demonic oppression or possession. This infestation we call death with its many manifestations affecting the entirety of our soul – mind, body, and spirit. Jesus alone has and can begin the healing process, and, within due time, He will permanently eradicate these dilemmas that each of us is faced with!

I See Dead People!

Apart from God whereby, mankind and men specifically, being left to their own devices, are prone to grossly and viciously misrepresent God as His purposed image-bears through their degenerate living. But how can a man represent their *Daddy,* in this instance, only their Creator, when they are, in fact, spiritually dead, cut off, and, therefore, no longer belonging to or is one with their *Dad.* But instead, He can only and rightly be viewed as their Creator (John 8:42-44). There are some undesirable people in this world, thereby leading some to describe these unfavorable lost souls as "walking zombies."

However, I caution you not to trivialize that serious spiritual dilemma and this Biblical truth: If you have not been *Born Again* or born from above by the Holy Spirit, you truly are amongst those in the class of "zombies;" you are indeed in the number paradoxically speaking of the living, but yet, you're walking dead. *Yes, I see dead people!...* You are dead in your unrepentant sins and dead because of sin (Ephesians 2:1-5; Colossians 2:13). While in this condition of spiritual death, divorced from God, and thus cut off from His very Essence – His *Nishmat Chayim – Breath of Divine Life,* one is severed from the source of all Truth, Life, Wisdom, and their Creator's purpose for His imagers (John 14:6; 1 Corinthians 1:30; Proverbs 2:6).

As seen with Adam and his wife, Eve, this spiritual separation from their *Dad* led to an inevitable decline and death sentence, as God's sustaining power was no longer present to guide, renew, and uphold *Man* to His standard of holiness or righteous living. Without *Daddy's Nishmat Chayim* – His essence of eternal life breathed in, or the Holy Spirit inhabiting *Man*, the human soul is left in a state of disrepair, spiritual decay, vulnerable to the influences of sin, darkness, and confusion. These are, in fact, dead people in our midst!

It is therefore inevitable that one will, in some manner or another, the severity varying with each of us, misuse and abuse themselves, need I say even misuse and abuse others! This is what dead people (zombies) do! This disconnection from God's life-giving Spirit leaves a void, which often results in destructive behavior, both toward oneself and others, as these lost souls grope for an unattainable meaning to life apart from their Creator (Romans 1:18-32; Psalm 81:12; Ephesian 4:19).

People, hear me clearly on this matter! Before one accepts Jesus as their Lord and Savior, and for certain, if He's outright rejected by an individual. No matter what "good" this person possesses or the "good" that they may do, they belong to their father, the Devil (John 8:44). In a very real sense, along with being sin-sick, *Man* can be likened to being hybrid creatures – genetically flawed individuals because of our unredeemed state, having been cut off from their Father and Creator.

And are, therefore, considered one with the Devil in this unholy and unnatural dysfunctional and toxic union that breeds or births death and destruction – the very essence of the Devil – their Daddy Dilemma! Yes, those of the world are one with him! Like Dad the Devil, so are his sons; his offspring like him; his imprint is upon them! Can't you see this in the gross immorality and killing observed all around us at the making of the dead!

Sin, or more precisely, spiritual death – the work of the Devil – begins to influence and affect us even before birth. Here's another truth that is often overlooked: demonic forces, evil spirits, or the powers of darkness are present from the moment we are conceived in our mothers' wombs, preparing to war against us when we are birth into Satan's world, who is currently the ruler over this cursed world (Ephesians 2:2; John 12:31; John 14:30). The moment we take our first breath as newborns, these spiritual forces of evil are poised to attack, whether near or far, seeking to further corrupt and destroy the potential child of God.

These assaults, both physical and psychological, can come at us from many sources – whether friends, "enemies," or even those closest to us, such as parents or relatives. They can also come at us through what we see, what we hear, how we are raised, or the influences we encounter in our homes and in the streets. These diabolical powers, acting through individuals and various mediums, work against our emotional and spiritual well-being, seeking to keep us away from the truth and *Saving Grace* of Jesus or to draw us away from God, our *Daddy*, and His love.

One's individual makeup will greatly influence how much of a beating or assault, whether physical, psychological, or even spiritual, one can withstand before breaking or sinking into despair, helplessness, and hopelessness. These attacks, whether long or short-term, can lead to significant emotional trauma, leaving a person damaged, depleted, and prone to becoming overly defensive or self-destructive. This physical and psychological damage can also result in an individual becoming dangerously insecure, therefore heightening their vulnerability and making it easier for others – who don't have this person's best interests at heart – to take advantage of their rejected and dejected state of mind.

Dead People Suffering From Trauma: A Dangerous and Potential Lethal Mix

Mankind merely attempting to function or live life in our simple brokenness, if I may term this description as such, is in bad enough condition as it is. However, when our brokenness is deepened by trauma, our dilemmas are magnified and intensified, bringing about utter amazement or even profound confusion to those of us observing trauma take on life in these individuals!

What we witnessed or that which may have been brought to our attention, in many cases, is, in fact, the result of a person who has suffered from something quite next-level distressing... a dangerous and potentially lethal mix. Subsequently, one who is subjected to and who is psychologically shaped under such hellish conditions is capable of birthing or demonstrating from their brokenness and trauma unimaginable and unfathomable fiendish or devilish acts of hideous violence or crimes against their fellow man that leave us speechless!

We, therefore, raise such questions as to why and how someone can do such horrific things. We feel this way because, inherently and in our humanity, along with reasonable saneness or sense of mind, we identify with this person as being one with us. This being the case, we feel deeply let down! This is an ultimate betrayal by such an individual who has committed such a horrible act or acts but not solely against their victim or victims, as others are indeed adversely affected – hence the ultimate betrayal! In our humanity and rationality, we hurt when others hurt; we are capable of empathizing with a victim's suffering while we question the perpetrator's state of mind and horrible violation of their fellow man. In some sense, we, too, may feel violated or victimized and yet again, thus causing one to feel betrayed.

The Impact of Moral Betrayal and Its Emotional Echoes

When we, as reasonable, sane individuals, one's age matters not, are betrayed or let down in a less obvious immoral manner, innately, we discern or know that we have been wronged. Clearly, I'm now not referring to letdowns or betrayals in the severity of murder and those affected by such violence or in the matters involving sexual abuse or brutality and other heinous acts against humanity that I've alluded to above. But rather, in the simple matter of moral betrayal thereby, our conscious or inner self alerting us of this wrong against us.

Consequently, a response to this betrayal is therefore provoked or incited within us. In the case described, it may be immediate or it could be delayed as you may have had to ponder what had occurred. I recognize that different emotions and depths of trauma may arise from these various letdowns or violations occurring against someone, which causes a need for deeper and further discussion. However, for this moment, I want to begin to delve in and work my way through situations that I believe have helped to form the emotional state of some or perhaps many females who feel *"Disdain For Daddy and Hatred of Men."*

A Look at Misogyny

In our society, a cry has been heard, and a siren has been blaring against what has been identified by more than a few women as a culture of misogyny that is at work against their equality with men. I personally don't believe men at large either wholeheartedly hate or are discriminating against women. That said, I will not dispute that there are misguided, broken, or emotionally damaged men who perhaps do... therefore, certainly a dilemma needing addressing and correction. Now, I'm not talking about sexually confused men – those struggling with the dilemma of gender identity as being the problem here, although undoubtedly, they can be included in this number.

But rather because of the misconduct, utter disrespect, and condescending views that too many heterosexual male influencers, specifically those identified as entertainers, have shown toward women. Such ignoble behavior, which I believe is, more often than not, displayed primarily in songs or portrayed on television, the movie screen, and now social media platforms, such disrespect and demeaning attitudes toward women that can rightly be viewed as misogyny. However, once again, I don't believe these condescending attitudes towards women represent a vast majority of men in North America but rather a troubled and misguided fraternity of a few men within this spiritually dysfunctional brotherhood of males who have large platforms or who hold positions of influence or wherever such flawed personalities may show up.

Just the same, this matter of misogyny may also be seen as being pervasive, resulting from a significant number of men, but if we are honest, also from a culture that likewise includes other women who objectify women for pleasure or monetary gain. We must also own this truth about this self-evident fact; countless women are likewise intentionally presenting themselves as immoral and immodest vixens or sexual objects to be desired. Whereas other women don't understand or are unaware of the Biblical concepts regarding how women are to be decent, conservative, or modest with their apparel and their manner of dressing – this being an outward appearance of a godly woman (1 Timothy 2:9,10; 1 Peter 3:3,4).

Therefore, it can very well be perceived by some women that misogyny is a widespread phenomenon or reality. Or it just might be one's personal experience being exaggerated. Or perhaps they have witnessed or know of such disrespect towards women; however, they choose to inflate the matter. Whatever the case, real or perceived, it should go without saying that hatred of any kind, condemnatory mischaracterization, and degrading speech or action directed towards any person is unacceptable, especially so for those who claim to be one with Jesus.

A Look at Misandry: This Assault of Satan's Agents Can't be Denied

Now, I want to also take a look at the matter of misandry – the hatred of men and, therefore, even utter disregard for Dad's or Husband's roles according to our Creator. Misandry, on the other hand, I personally believe has become a concerning matter. There may be actual proof and data to support my claim. For certain, there is empirical evidence that strongly suggests that women's hatred of men is factually on the rise. Furthermore, I am also inclined to believe that the failures of men and daddies, or the lack of godly men and/or misguided boys their age mattering not, is the root of this problem or dilemma! This has caused a greater number, and perhaps a significantly larger number, of women who actually have disdain or hatred for men than what men are accused of having toward women.

Perhaps we can see eye-to-eye on the following matters if, by chance, you are not inclined to embrace my position thus far: I find it quite bizarre and even alarming that these are actual matters of discussion today. Nevertheless, now continuing, I associate this rising cause of contempt that girls and women, and I will add some males, have toward men or even boys is ultimately and mainly because of what I have presented as the **Daddy Dilemma!**

Because of this Daddy Dilemma, one thing is for sure: the Satanic realm is at work, whether through misogyny or misandry or otherwise, sowing division and discord between modern-day Adams and Eves, men and women, boys and girls! Satan's spiritual influence at work through his satanic hordes has many of us (men and women, boys and girls) exactly where he wants us, divided, confused, and with hostility, at odds with one another!

I will further my thoughts on this matter of the *Daddy Dilemma*; however, before doing so, I want to elaborate on how I've arrived at my position on this matter of the emergence of misandry. For starters, I've never been amongst a group of men nor heard or seen such conduct from a boy or man that indicates or suggests they hate or have disdain for women. However, a man's or boy's disgusting and degrading treatment of girls or women is a different matter.

"Black Lives Matter:" Read In Between the Lines

Unless your head has been under a rock or you don't watch mainstream television or mediums of the like. You have undoubtedly seen or heard from platforms like feminist groups, lesbian women alliances, or other like organizations, *Feminist Majority Foundation, The Reformation Project, Black Lives Matter,* and their supporters with their unconventional or delusional views who challenge Scripture or reject them altogether. And who are, therefore, hell-bent on their radical demonic agendas to reorder God-ordained societal norms where families are to be headed by loving, godly husbands and supported by their loving, godly wives; women, according to the Bible, who are without question equal to their husbands.

Such women who serve in their God-purposed roles as being submissive and supportive to their spouses in their position as head of the home, while they show mutual respect for one another in their divinely designed functions as husband and wife (1 Corinthians 11:3; Colossians 3:18; Ephesians 6:1-3), they too are faced with their unique challenges. Namely, being challenged by those (feminist) who claim that their "traditional" way of living is antiquated and oppressive. They all but advocate that these wives should rebel against their husbands or God's patriarchal system. Women, stand your ground; honor your husbands and your God!

There are self-proclaimed Misandrists and others who may not embrace this description, whose aim, however, is none other than to "dismantle" or "disrupt" their so-called "Western ideal of family and its patriarchal system." Read this charter for "Black Lives Matter," furthermore, be sure to also read between the lines. The first half of this charter or mission statement doesn't concern me as much as the latter half.

"What We Believe" – Est. 7/13/13

"Four years ago (7/13/13), what is now known as the Black Lives Matter Global Network began to organize. It started out as a chapter-based, member-led organization whose mission was to build local power and to intervene when violence was inflicted on Black communities by the state and vigilantes.

In the years since, we've committed to struggling together and to imagining and creating a world free of anti-Blackness, where every Black person has the social, economic, and political power to thrive.

Black Lives Matter began as a call to action in response to state-sanctioned violence and anti-Black racism. Our intention from the very beginning was to connect Black people from all over the world who have a shared desire for justice to act together in their communities. The impetus for that commitment was, and still is, the rampant and deliberate violence inflicted on us by the state.

Enraged by the death of Trayvon Martin and the subsequent acquittal of his killer, George Zimmerman, and inspired by the 31-day takeover of the Florida State Capitol by POWER U and the Dream Defenders, we took to the streets. A year later, we set out together on the Black Lives Matter Freedom Ride to Ferguson, in search of justice for Mike Brown and all of those who have been torn apart by state-sanctioned violence and anti-Black racism. Forever changed, we returned home and began building the infrastructure for the Black Lives Matter Global Network, which, even in its infancy, has become a political home for many.

Ferguson helped to catalyze a movement to which we've all helped give life. Organizers who call this network home have ousted anti-Black politicians, won critical legislation to benefit Black lives, and changed the terms of the debate on Blackness around the world. Through movement and relationship building, we have also helped catalyze other movements and shifted culture with an eye toward the dangerous impacts of anti-Blackness.

These are the results of our collective efforts.

The Black Lives Matter Global Network is as powerful as it is because of our membership, our partners, our supporters, our staff, and you. Our continued commitment to liberation for all Black people means we are continuing the work of our ancestors and fighting for our collective freedom because it is our duty.

Every day, we recommit to healing ourselves and each other, and to co-creating alongside comrades, allies, and family a culture where each person feels seen, heard, and supported.

We acknowledge, respect, and celebrate differences and commonalities.

We work vigorously for freedom and justice for Black people and, by extension, all people.

We intentionally build and nurture a beloved community that is bonded together through a beautiful struggle that is restorative, not depleting.

We are unapologetically Black in our positioning. In affirming that Black Lives Matter, we need not qualify our position. To love and desire freedom and justice for ourselves is a prerequisite for wanting the same for others.

We see ourselves as part of the global Black family, and we are aware of the different ways we are impacted or privileged as Black people who exist in different parts of the world.

[It is from this point on that the wording in this charter shifts. As an Orthodox, Traditional, or Conservative Christian, this language brings me concern.]

We are guided by the fact that all Black lives matter, regardless of actual or perceived sexual identity, gender identity, gender expression, economic status, ability, disability, religious beliefs or disbeliefs, immigration status, or location.

We make space for transgender brothers and sisters to participate and lead.

We are self-reflexive and do the work required to **dismantle cisgender privilege** *and uplift Black trans folk, especially Black trans women who continue to be disproportionately impacted by trans-antagonistic violence.*

We build a space that affirms Black women and is free from sexism, **misogyny,** *and environments in which* **men are centered.**

We practice empathy. We engage comrades with the intent to learn about and connect with their contexts.

We make our spaces family-friendly and enable parents to fully participate with their children. **We dismantle the patriarchal practice** *that requires mothers to work "double shifts" so that they can mother in private even as they participate in public justice work.*

We disrupt the Western-prescribed nuclear family structure *requirement by supporting each other as extended families and "villages" that collectively care for one another, especially our children, to the degree that mothers, parents, and children are comfortable.*

We foster a queer-affirming network. *When we gather, we do so with the intention of freeing ourselves from* **the tight grip of heteronormative**

*thinking, or rather, **the belief that all in the world are heterosexual*** *(unless s/he or they disclose otherwise).*

We cultivate an intergenerational and communal network free from ageism. We believe that all people, regardless of age, show up with the capacity to lead and learn.

We embody and practice justice, liberation, and peace in our engagements with one another."

This original document has since been deleted from their website and significantly modified [Black Lives Matter Charter, dated 7/13/2013; Founders: Alicia Garza, Patrisse Cullors, Ayo aka Opal Tometi].

In other words, what I see this organization and its partners or supporters of like mind are saying is as follows: What God has to say in the Bible about how He has ordained or created men and women to function in God-ordained home matters not to such individuals, groups, or organizations. They have, therefore, redefined the meaning of a family and marriage as seen in their own eyes – hence ***Individualism, Secular Humanism, Moral Relativism,* or *Existentialism*.**

Intersex Individuals: They Are Unique

Satan, having blinded and deceived God's beloved creatures, also resulting from their rejecting of Biblical truth or their *Daddy,* God Himself. With their degenerate and humanistic worldview, thereby incorporating their relative reasoning, they are also medically and surgically corrupting or perverting their clearly identifiable biological gender uniqueness – being either male or female away from that which was distinctively purposed by their Creator at birth. What an alarming dilemma God's children or the

Church are faced with. However, the Church must also grapple with the unusual and **unique** dilemma and rare challenge before us in which a small minority of people have chromosomal or testosterone abnormalities, whereby such individuals are medically described as **"Intersex."**

In a Christian context and from the understanding that I've gained, the medical term **"Intersex"** is understood as referring to individuals who are born, in such rare occurrences, with physical or biological sex characteristics that do not correspond to typical definitions of male or female or that perfect state of *Man* before the *Edenic Fall.* These abnormalities may or may not be readily observed when a child is born. Nevertheless, these malformations do not preclude these individuals' distinct biological identities as existing or being conceived or created as male and female (Genesis 1:2; Gen. 2:22-24; Mark 10:6).

As for a Christian's perspective on this matter, these variations are to be seen as part of the reality of living in a fallen world, where physical and biological anomalies occur as a result of the bodily corruption of mankind introduced through sin. Far from being the norm, **Intersex** conditions are an inherent reflection of the difficulty within *Man's* state of temporal existence, a unique dilemma in a world that is awaiting restoration or its redemption.

As children of God, we must recognize the dignity and value of all people created in God's image who have their varying challenges as we also remain mindful of the impact of the fallen state of creation or sin's effects upon and/or within each of us (Romans 8:19-22). With regards to the LGBQTIA + community. I will argue that "I" in this acronym, meaning **Intersex** individuals, should be excluded. Unlike those who have chosen their sexual orientation or sexual preferences, **Intersex** individuals had no say or choice in the matter; they were, in fact, born uniquely.

Regarding others within the *Lettered Community*, your situation is different. However, your dilemma is not unlike other sinners. We all have to war against our sin-nature, or sinful dispositions, inclinations, or bends (Romans 7:18-19; Galatians 5:17). Therefore, one can choose to heed or surrender to God's message of deliverance and Redemption through Jesus (Romans 10:9-10), or one can choose to remain in your practice or lifestyle of sin (Hebrews 10:26-27; 1 John 3:8). God loves you as you are (John 3:16; Romans 5:8).

However, to become His child, you cannot remain as you are (John 1:12-13; 2 Corinthians 5:17). It is for sin that Jesus, our *Ultimate Difference Maker*, came into this world, that we may be delivered from the grip or *Stronghold* of sin, having dominion over our lives (John 8:34-36; Romans 6:6-7). To remain as you are, one with sinful practices, or your Dad – the Devil Dilemma, this will not be without consequences (Romans 6:23; John 8:44). Even so, God's condemnation is already upon you (John 3:18; Romans 1:18-20).

That said, I am nevertheless convinced that there are indeed such delusional, broken, lost, or perverted souls who are the driving force behind the narratives being pushed and the horn blaring regarding misandry and the disruption or dismantling of the Bible's divinely designated role and function of man and woman or husband and wife. Furthermore, these misguided false teachers also seek to rewrite or redefine God's order and command for a husband and wife to join Him as His agents and children for the purpose of procreation.

No matter one's fallen condition or state of mind, God wants to deliver His offspring who are stubbornly rebellious against His divine purpose from the stronghold of Satan's lies and deceptions, which is leading them to destruction. That He, their loving Creator, may regenerate and restore His lost children to Himself that they may call to Him... *Daddy!* Even so, their *Divine Difference Maker* (1 Corinthians 6:9-11; Romans 1:18-32)!

Contempt for Men: My Personal Experience

I have shared empirical evidence involving those who resist God and His design for *Man*. Now, I will present my personal experiences or encounters that I had with four females who opposed and had contempt for me for no other reason than I was a male imager of my *Daddy*. I will provide the details of three unrelated events in the order that they occurred. From the first encounter to the last experience, perhaps 15 to 20 years span these unusual and, at the time, surprising experiences that I was confronted with. With the last event occurring perhaps some five years or so ago:

At the time of the first encounter, I was a Detective employed by the City of Durham Police Department. Bear in mind this was perhaps 3 decades ago and maybe some 20 years before the "Me Too Movement." During this era, the "LGBTQIA+ community" did not have any noticeable public traction, unlike today. Much has changed in the world since then! During that time and even now, I would graciously and respectfully address any female, and certainly, if I'd forgotten their name, by such titles as Ma'am, Dear, Love, Hun, Babe, etc.

Correspondingly, there are times that I am addressed in the same manner by a female who is being cordial and who may barely know me, if not by a complete stranger; with these expressions, I have absolutely no objection. I embrace such word choice from a female as one who was simply being friendly and who felt comfortable with me. As adults, we know when someone is being flirtatious or inappropriate by using such expressions. This was by no means the case with me in this personal experience that I will now share.

There was this one and only time that a female who also was a Police Officer took exception to me addressing her as "Dear." When this officer was of equal rank with me and when she acquired a slightly higher ranking than me, I remember holding meaningful and cordial conversations with her. This may have been closer to 35 years ago, and at the time, her sexual lifestyle choice was not something that I was aware of or had given thought to.

As far as I was concerned, she was just, ordinary good people. However, a decade or so later, she now holds the rank of Lieutenant or Captain, rankings significantly higher than my professional status as a Detective. She was then well known to have a reputation as being a difficult person; I'm now being nice with this characterization. I was not under her direct command; however, she was considered my superior.

On this particular day, as we were walking down the hall, about to pass one another. Not giving thought to the matter, I kindly and respectfully addressed her by saying, "Good morning, Dear," as she and I were now within greeting distance. However, she abruptly and surprisingly snapped back at me! What she did not do was acknowledge my greeting. Nor did she professionally say to me that she would prefer for me to address her by her rank, which I would have respectfully been accommodating.

To my surprise and somewhat dismay, I encountered that unfavorable side of her that I'd heard about and, from later observation, had discerned within her disposition. Her immediate come-back to my greeting went along these lines: "Tony" or perhaps "Detective," I don't appreciate you addressing me as Dear! That's disrespectful!" Her follow-up comment heightened the moment and, in a way, allowed me to see into the questionable manner in which her mind was working.

In her conclusion, she said, "What you said to me can be considered inappropriate and sexual harassment." I remember thinking, "You are my superior; therefore, how can you make such an outlandish accusation and threat." It would have been absolutely foolish of me to intend anything beyond my casual and friendly greeting and acknowledgment of her.

During this time, the "LGBQTIA+ Community's" agenda was beginning to gain some footing, even within the Police Department. Nevertheless, this was before Ellen DeGeneres "came out of the closet." However, when she did "come out of the closet," this one act of open rebellion and defiance against her Creator really galvanized and gave the "queer" movement unrelenting momentum; its effects have since become entrenched throughout the so-called civilized or Western world. It would be perhaps 2 decades later when the Supreme Court would legalize self-proclaimed "Gay Marriages," which was wholeheartedly embraced by then-President Barack Obama. What a dilemma the church would now be faced with!

Politics aside, Scripturally speaking, this was another egregious and significantly cultural and even globally impacting moment and sinister satanic movement or attack. An act of ultimate defiance against our God and Creator that had now been full-throated, embraced by many belonging to their father, the Devil. And "legally" endorsed and given credence by the many ruling authorities of this fallen world, who unwittingly or not were influenced by the forces of spiritual wickedness that hold sway over its inhabitants or such ones belonging to Satan's kingdom (Ephesians 6:12; Leviticus 18:22; Romans 1:25-27).

As for this female officer who out-ranked me professionally and others who are of the same mind – one with this sinful queer lifestyle choice; now, broadly speaking, all sexually broken and deceived creatures, in most cases, will attempt to defend the practice of their dishonorable lifestyles when threaten or challenged.

This defensive response being the case with this officer in displaying workplace dominance as her strategy; she having been led astray by her longing to feel or experience a semblance of love and unquestionable acceptance on her own terms. Therefore, felt that it was necessary to challenge, silence, and subtly threaten me because she had disdain for my greeting her as "Dear," if not me personally, as a male imager of God, a direct contradiction of that which she chose to now image. Yes, at this point, her "Butch" persona had become more evident to me; could this have also been the reason she objected to my recognition of her as "Dear"… even though Dear is gender-neutral?

The tone and intent of this officer. With like-minded individuals utilizing these kinds of ploys or attacks, herein, a claim to be offended, being defensive against their drummed-up opposition, and even hatred towards those who do not agree with their lifestyle is more prevalent today. This kind of confrontational or defensive stance has now been heightened. Indeed, such actions have become a common tactic, with there being other methods utilized by this dysfunctional *Community* or family to defend their perverted positions while silencing or having their oppositions "canceled."

Conversely, in their push to be relevant or accepted, they aim to delegitimize what God has identified as a God-ordained family and the proper conduct that a male and female, His imagers, are to demonstrate. And without question, those within His holy family or kingdom – His children or the Church, even so, the very Bride of Christ who is to be solely and wholly committed to Him are to demonstrate. As Jesus is Holy, so has He called His *Bride* – the Church to be holy – no longer practicing sinful lifestyle choices (Leviticus 19:2; 2 Corinthians 11:2; Revelation 19: 7-9; Rev. 21:1,2).

With regards to one being holy, I remind you that this does not mean that a person is perfect or without sin. Holiness means to be one with God. To be covenanted with Him and sanctified or set apart for His purpose or will for one's life as provided in the Bible for those who belong to the family of *Dad, our Difference Maker.* It is the child of God who has committed their hearts to God, their *Daddy.* And, therefore, does not practice or willingly permit sinful or immoral behavior to be identified therewith. For this child of God, sin no longer has dominion over their life; instead, they live to honor their Father in and through their bodies; this is holy living unto *Daddy* as His imagers and children (Romans 6:12-14; Romans 12: 1,2; 1 Corinthians 6:19,20).

For the record, I did not seek verifiable proof to identify this individual, my former co-worker, as being one with this dysfunctional and delusional *Community.* However, at that time and currently, mere empirical data can enable one to arrive at many reliable and reasonable conclusions about others. It is also significantly plausible that this person came at me with the visceral fervor that she displayed because she also knew that I was a Christian. However, perhaps, more threatening to her way of thinking and agenda, that I had become a preacher of the *Good News of Jesus*.

Unlike today, three decades ago and unquestionably beyond, the Universal Church of God almost unanimously opposed unconventional life practices, homosexual lifestyle choices, or fornication, a word encompassing all sexual practices occurring outside of God's design for marriage. Then I heard about the dilemma of "Gender Dysphoria" and Species Dysphoria."

Gender and Species Dysphoria: A New Phenomenon and Perversion of God's People

Now, as for the disturbing matter of so-called "Gender Dysphoria," this was not a topic heard about in mainstream media, for many, myself included, had no idea this was even a brewing dilemma.

What is Gender Dysphoria:

Gender dysphoria is said by the ***so-called experts*** (false teachers or prophets or teachers, 2 Peter 2:1) to be a psychological condition where an individual experiences significant distress or discomfort because their gender identity (their internal sense of being male, female, or another gender) <u>does not align with their sex "assigned at birth</u>."

Let's make something clear, an individual is generally born either male – XY Chromosome or female – XX Chromosome. One is not assigned a sex; a person is either a biological male or female.

These "experts" contend this incongruence can lead to emotional, psychological, and physical challenges, particularly if the individual feels their body does not reflect ***their true self.*** These "experts" say, Gender dysphoria is defined by the presence of distress or impairment, not simply by a mismatch between gender identity and assigned sex.

Symptoms so, they say, can include a strong desire to be treated as another gender, discomfort with one's physical characteristics, and a wish to alter one's body to align with their gender identity. The "experts" continue that these conditions affect children, adolescents, and adults differently, often manifesting as a preference for gender roles traditionally associated with another gender in children and deeper emotional or physical distress in adults.

Because these "experts" do not acknowledge *Man's* sin condition or spiritual warfare, they say treatment often involves a combination of therapy, social support, and, for some, medical interventions like hormone therapy or surgeries to align their body with their gender identity. It's important to note that not everyone whose gender identity differs from their ***assigned sex*** experiences dysphoria, and respect and acceptance are crucial for supporting individuals navigating this experience.

As for Species Dysphoria:

So, the "experts" claim it is another "psychological condition" in which, mirroring Gender Dysphoria, an individual experiences discomfort or distress because they feel their true identity does not align with being human. People with species dysphoria often believe they are, in essence, another species, such as an animal or mythical being, and may feel a strong connection to or identification with that species.

This condition is distinct from gender dysphoria, as it involves a mismatch between one's self-perception and humanity rather than gender identity.

While species dysphoria is not widely recognized in diagnostic manuals like the DSM-5, some individuals describe it as a deeply personal experience that can affect their mental and emotional well-being. It may be associated with broader identity or existential concerns rather than physical incongruence.

These "experts" conclude support for those with species dysphoria typically involves exploring these feelings through therapy, though societal understanding and resources for this condition are more limited compared to gender dysphoria. [*Information obtained through ChatGPT.*]

I say again, much has changed in our world as a result of many who have shown disdain and even hatred toward my *Daddy* and their Creator – who is **the Way, the Truth, and the Life;** it is He who seeks to bring deliverance from lies and deception by leading all to Himself through Jesus (John 14:6; John 1:14; John 8:31,32; John 18:36-38)! The Bible says that in the *Last Days,* many will believe lies and deceiving spirits and, thereby, be given over to strong delusions (2 Thessalonians 2:9-12; 1 Timothy 4:1). Such people may very well need therapy. However, they surely need Jesus our Healer – the Great Physician (Matthew 9:12; Luke 4:18)!

Regarding my subsequent encounter, this experience involved a young lady who, sadly, did not possess a positive view of her biological father; she actually had disdain for him. While functioning in my line of work as a Police Officer. I remember being dispatched to a call regarding a domestic disturbance located on Fayetteville St. near Dunbar St. in Durham, N.C. The details of this incident have now escaped my memory.

However, I recall this young lady having a dispute with her "female partner" about not being allowed to enter the apartment. I'm sure I remember this occasion for these reasons: This may have been the first time that I'd responded to a call where "partners" were of the same sex, and the young lady whom I was addressing in this ordeal may have been a teenager or barely 20 years of age.

When I responded to calls classified as domestic disturbances of whatever the underlying nature, I did not simply offer professional advice and then went on my way. It was my practice as I was concerned for all involved to attempt to determine the primary reason or factors that led to the need for police intervention. It became apparent that this young lady was not going to be granted access to the house.

Therefore, in an attempt to provide her with guidance and to console her. Even so, me getting to know more about this person and her way of thinking, and even how she came to embrace the lifestyle as a lesbian. I made reference to her dad or asked her a question about him. Now, as for what was perhaps the standout reason for me recalling this event on that night: At my mentioning her dad, this young lady responded forcefully and passionately to me, "I hate my Daddy!" I don't recall anything further that she nor I said after her angry outburst.

What I do recall is feeling her pain... while my mind also wondered, throughout my work shift, what happened that caused this young lady to feel such profound hatred towards her dad. When I'd given thought to the relationship that I would have had with my daughter if God had gifted me with one. Our bond would have been unbreakable! She would have become the reason for my being and the apple of my eye! Therefore, this young lady's anger and hatred toward her dad were troubling and unfathomable to me.

Perhaps I was also able to recall this brief encounter that has been etched in my memory with this young lady, is because I also once hated and had disdain for the man who I once identified with as being my biological reason for existing – hence, loosely speaking, my daddy. More will be said on this matter and my personal Daddy Dilemma to include the other men, also dilemmas central to my life soon enough.

This last account and encounter that I will now share involved two young ladies, who I believe were high school-aged, but the incident did not involve my direct engagement with them. As it were, I was sitting on a table at a local lake. These two females were quite friendly toward one another, there being nothing unusual about their interaction. However, as they walked in the direction of where I was sitting, we were now holding brief eye contact as they carried on in a playful and jovial manner. One of the young ladies then communicated these words, which were directed at me, "We hate men!" as they strolled off in laughter. Other than sharing my bewilderment by the statement directed at me, I don't recall any thoughts that may have entered my mind. However, their thoughts were made abundantly clear to me, "They hated men!"

I think it goes without saying that young ladies and women having disdain and hatred of men and even their own Dads is not something that has just sprung up in isolation. Or that this is something new only to our era. However, I raise the question: what accounts for the prevalence of such raw emotions being shared and negative dispositions by so many females toward men and even one's Dad for such times as ours?

I will now submit the word *attitude* to distinguish between such females with attitudes, in contrast to females who have genuine reasons to feel as they do toward men, as observed from the anguish that is brought forth from within their soul from the mere thought or mention of the word dad. Instead of this designation – Dad, provoking fond memories of unconditional love, fun times, acceptance, and security, the name Dad, for many, has become a trigger word that stirs up all kinds of negative emotions, not only for their dads but men in general.

In times past, some females who had such troubling *emotions,* this being the distinction from those females with *attitudes,* kept their emotions or thoughts to themselves or were prohibited from freely expressing their feelings. Due to cultural or familial norms, I posit that such emotions or attitudes have not, until recently, been largely a social concern to be openly expressed.

However, now prompted by a cultural shift away from or defiance of God by those who are pushing their own agendas in opposition to Biblical norms. Their upside-down social construct, movement, or even satanic takeover, having significantly seized momentum in the United States and abroad, has given rise to this segment of our society who have unjust and even manufactured disdain or hatred for men, comprising of one's own daddy, need I say to include God Himself, is no longer taboo or seen as disrespectful. But it is now encouraged! With that having been said, where dads have been a dilemma and the cause for dilemmas in their child[ren] life, one's voice should never have been silenced or be hushed from expressing their hurt and feelings caused by their Daddy Dilemma or some other male being the reason for their dilemmas.

Nevertheless, I am inclined, as stated, to believe that currently, the loudest voices and outcries are from those women in particular and *self-proclaimed others* with misguided attitudes and agendas! As for those who are genuinely crying out, broken, and hurting, some have been embraced and perhaps manipulated to make them feel that they should be or are one with those women or *others* (the LGBQTIA+ community) with attitudes who have an agenda that stands in opposition to the will of their Creator. Just the same, I will keep the question before us, although having been answered, as to "Why now and the prevalence of such feelings."

I am aware that additional reasons can be offered for our cultural shifts and norms being redefined. However, there is one underlying and undeniable reason or root cause for such emotional distress and bad attitudes; the answer or solution resides in *The Divine Daddy Dilemma*. Meaning because our *Dad* or Creator is no longer being embraced by many, nor His *Truth* and *Way* wholeheartedly embraced or lived out by far too many of His own children who are supposed to be His imagers. This has led to the biological "Daddy Dilemma" and subsequent social and moral ills we now face within families and with many individually!

Lest we forget, the origin of *Man's* dilemma is tied to the Ultimate Dilemma – the Devil himself, who opposes all that represents our Father or Creator's *Holiness, Truth,* and *Life-essence*! Like their Daddy – the Devil, his sons and daughters who oppose and reject God, their Creator's *Way* unto holiness and righteous living, will instead follow after the nature of their Daddy Dilemma – the Devil, which can only lead to chaos, hurt, meanness, hatred, discontent, confusion and so on (Romans 1:28-32; Galatians 5:19-21). These are fruits or the byproducts of death (John 8:44; 1 John 3:8-10; Matthew 13:40-42; Matt. 25: 41)!

But the fruit of the Spirit is love, joy, peace, long-suffering, kindness, goodness, faithfulness, gentleness, self-control. Against such, there is no law." (*NKJV*)

The nine attributes of the Fruit of the Spirit are:

1. **Love** – Unselfish, sacrificial, and unconditional care for others.

2. **Joy** – A deep, abiding gladness in the Lord that is not dependent on circumstances.

3. **Peace** – Inner calmness and harmony, trusting God in all situations.

4. **Long-suffering** (Patience) – The ability to endure difficulties and wait on God without complaining.

5. **Kindness** – Showing compassion and care for others in words and actions.

6. **Goodness** – Living a life of moral integrity and generosity.

7. **Faithfulness** – Being reliable, loyal, and trustworthy in our relationship with God and others.

8. **Gentleness** – Exercising humility and meekness without weakness.

9. **Self-control** – Mastery over one's desires and actions, being disciplined by the Spirit.

These qualities reflect the character of Christ and are evidence of the Holy Spirit working in a *Believer's* life.

CHAPTER 3

Why Now and The Prevalence of Such Feelings

Gospel musician and singer-songwriter Fred Hammond sings a heart-moving interlude to Kirk Franklin's song, "Truth," that powerfully magnifies the Daddy Dilemma and its effect on their offspring. The words found therein profoundly provide additional insight into the answer to my question, "Why Now and The Prevalence of Such Feelings" of disdain for Daddy and hatred of men. Listen closely to these heart-wrenching words:

*"There's a **hole** in my soul*
That won't heal
*And there's a **rage** and a **pain***
Even now, I still feel
And even though I'm a man (woman)
Still, I don't understand
But that's what happens when you don't have a father
That's what happens when you don't have a father."

Here is something that needs to be acknowledged: One not having a Father is not merely his physical absence from his child[ren] or family, which is a major dilemma. That said, the physical essence of a dad can very well be present in the home, and yet he is absent in that he does not adequately provide for his child, neither meet their emotional needs nor lead his offspring to the *Source* – God their *Daddy*, where their spiritual needs may be attended to. Although having a "good" daddy is better than having no daddy at all, nonetheless, as I have mentioned, God our Father desires that godly and not solely good dads be in their rightful position or orientation with Him.

So that we, as men, may operate in our rightful stations before our families as godly dads and husbands – spiritual and physical protectors and caregivers are two such stations. When and where this is not the case, men or dads being one or in their rightful position with God our Creator, all sorts and degrees of hell or atrocities can overtake one's home and mankind societally. This we are seeing! And some have or are experiencing first-hand!

Starting from within the homes where godly dads are absent, developmental, psychological, and spiritual issues will very likely plague our offspring in varying manners or degrees. Let me emphasize such dilemmas arising apart from trauma that a child can very well experience merely because their dad or protector is not in his rightful place! This Daddy Dilemma will also very likely, in varying measures furthermore, mentally and emotionally handicap or frustrate the mother of our children.

When daddies and husbands are not rightly oriented with God! This hole within a child's soul because Daddy isn't there, make no mistake about it, can also be experienced by the mother of his offspring. Fatherless children and their mothers can or will experience this Daddy Dilemma or void within their souls because our Creator's order for the family is missing, and an essential part – Daddy!

Mama Drama - Because of this, Daddy Dilemma!

This condition of a mother (possessing a hole in her soul or void), which will very likely be coupled with tremendous hurt and perhaps the feeling of abandonment and betrayal, can also lead to what I have termed **Mama Drama because of this, Daddy Dilemma!** Subsequently, the child[ren] who is abandoned by their dads to the care of their single mother, approximately 25 million children, now have to struggle within their minds and try to make sense of why their Daddy isn't there to love them. [U.S. Census Bureau for the statistic about children born to unwedded parents.]

Many fatherless children are then left attempting to navigate an oftentimes challenging home life, and all this entails because their mom has also been mentally and emotionally handicapped because of their Dad's intentional disappearance, absence, or abandonment (1 Timothy 5:8; Colossians 3:21).

I will now say of the matter, in view of those men who purposefully never showed up (MAA), wherein neglecting their paternal responsibilities or who deposited their seed in a consensual sexual situation or not and then vanished. Or those who abandoned their families are, in my judgment, unworthy and unfit to be called, or identified as a dad or recognized as a father, hence a dilemma of far-reaching consequences!

It is, therefore, because of my unique personal situations regarding such Daddy Dilemmas that such men are termed by me as merely as **Biological Reason for Being or Paternal Progenitors.** They do not deserve to have bestowed upon them the honored titles of Dad or Father; instead, this phrasing provided is what I have found fitting to call such unworthy individuals. But, of course, you may have your own descriptors. Under said circumstances, tragic it is, single mothers, are now forced to perform the parenting responsibilities that were designed by our Creator for two – a biological dad and mom, fashioned by God as complementary opposites to care for their offspring and gift from their Creator and God.

The Weaponization of Sex

These two – dad and mom, having uniquely joined together sexually as designed by our Creator to bring forth a child[ren] through what should have been marriage; herein is only sexual relations permitted. It is also important that you understand the following sinister truth: Sexual relations outside of marriage is Satan's tool to *biologically weaponize Man* in order to ultimately pervert and destroy individuals and families.

Hence the **Weaponization of Sex,** in which, catastrophically, many are held captive or dead in their sins, who are spiritually blind or undeveloped as children of God, through carnal thinking, being fleshly driven, find delight in such satanic, demeaning, and disastrous indulgence (1 Corinthians 3:1-3). I, too, was once numbered amongst Satan's agents as a *sexualized weapon of mass destruction!* If you are a child of God, you can not allow your passions to have mastery over you. If you are engaging in sexual relations outside of marriage, you have become a tool or weapon for Satan (Romans 6:12-18).

Furthermore, God has purposed that parents, through this holy union of husband and wife, are to remain together faithfully until death due them part, at which time this covenant relationship between these two and God is then ended, completed, or perfected on this side of heaven (Matthew 19:6; Malachi 2:13-16; Ephesians 5:31-33; Psalms 127:3-5).

In light of and because of the *Weaponization of Sex*, **40%** of the children born in the United States are born to unwedded parents. [U.S. Census Bureau for the statistic about children born to unwedded parents.]

With an estimate of **1/3** of children not knowing who their father is. [The Pew Research Center and the American Journal of Human Biology.]

And with as high as **10%** of individuals discovering their paternal biological origins through home DNA testing, a matter in which I'm intimately acquainted. What a dilemma!

Children raised under such dysfunctional *Daddy Dilemmas,* this having been my personal experience and upbringing; I'm, therefore, at liberty to designate such men as I saw it, see it, and lived it, my (our) ***Biological Reason for Being or Paternal Progenitor***. Even so, because this estranged and fragmented household falls short of God's ideal family, it is, therefore, abnormal or even dysfunctional. This is not to suggest that God has abandoned such a family. Or that great things or people cannot arise above and out of such an environment. On the contrary, many people have, and this includes my mother's children. I point this out in my previous book. However, I also mention because of the Daddy Dilemma within our home that, each of my mother's children, in differing manners and degrees, were emotionally and psychologically affected.

Is what I have mentioned reason alone for a child to grow to have disdain for their dads or hatred for men? Well, each of us is different in our makeup, and our thresholds or breaking points are not across the board the same. This means that each person responds differently to the challenges they face, and therefore, the outcome – resulting from cause and effect, including the Daddy Dilemma – can vary significantly. So, it cannot be said with certainty that a child who grows up experiencing personal Daddy Dilemmas or situations like the ones discussed is immune to hating men or harboring disdain for their dad.

However, it is crucial to recognize that these struggles are not merely the result of personal experience but also stem from our fallen nature. We are born into sin, each with our own unique battles to face. Along with our inherent flaws, there are unseen spiritual forces at work, ready to influence us from the very moment we draw our first breath. The devil, in his various forms – whether through satanic influences, demonic oppression, or evil spirits – seeks to attack and disrupt our lives. These forces may be near or far, but they are always poised to come against us. At the moment of birth and throughout our lives, they are there, waiting to prey on our vulnerabilities, intensifying our struggles, and seeking to sow hatred, confusion, and division.

Now, heightening or making more egregious the Daddy Dilemma. I will provide an additional reason why an individual may most assuredly hate or have disdain for men, including one's dad. However, regarding this matter of dad, and from what's been stated up to this point, I am merely nominally acknowledging one as a dad. Now, as for a daddy who may have been present or not in the home of their child. Or perhaps a close male relative, family friend, father figure, or some other trusted male under whose care the child (their age is now irrelevant) was tragically violated by this person.

This individual or even one's dad, having sexually violated the child who was under their care or watch, such a horrific act is certain to inflict psychological or even physical trauma upon said individual that cannot be measured. Far too often, this is a recurring and prevalent theme and even demonic attack that too many innocent offspring of God have been met with and overtaken by!

In occurrences such as this, it is easy to understand why one may grow up, or a person abused in this manner has strong disdain and hatred of boys and men, as well as having other emotional or developmental dilemmas. Again, Satan cannot come against God, his Creator. Therefore, mankind, in our fallen condition, sin within each of us, any of us, even so, the child of God, who is not watchful and prayerful, can be utilized by Satan as his agents of great harm and destruction to one another! In this misuse and abuse of ourselves and others, this is the only way that Satan troubles God.

There is no need to describe how these abuses may have come about. Many of us likely know of someone who has been transgressed against in this manner and are, therefore, familiar with their sorrowful story. Or it just may be that you have experienced such betrayal of trust and unspeakable hurt and devastation yourself from such a male who became one with the Devil unto your hurt and this ultimate violation of *sex being weaponized!*

Vengeance Belongs to God

These males, in most cases, are unwittingly being utilized by the Devil, even though they are also acting out of their sinful passions and own volition (James 1:14,15). Coupled with and through adept or clever demonic influence, it is also likely that, in extreme cases, this being the highest level of bodily corruption, one knowingly or not gives themself over or opens oneself up to demonic possession (Ephesians 6:12; 1 Peter 5:8,9). While in this self-imposed condition, mankind has been led to commit such monstrous acts of destructive violence and other atrocities against their fellow man and imagers of God.

That said, no matter the inducement or motivation behind such wicked acts! These males are akin to the Devil, utilized by him as *biological weapons* to carry out his spiritual war tactics and PsyOps – psychological operations, thereby sowing mental and emotional chaos and destruction upon the souls of others. As for these malevolent men, who are unrepentant, hence one with the Devil, spiritually given over to their sinful ways, they will be held accountable before God (James 1:14,15). God has stated clearly that vengeance is His (Romans 12:19; Deuteronomy 32:35; 2 Thessalonians 1:6; Proverbs 20:22. Also read Mark 5:1-20; Luke 8:2; Romans 6:12,13; Ephesians 6:12; Luke 4:1-13)!

People, hear me clearly on this: In this darkened world complete with sin-sick and traumatized people, the horrors we see and experience are inevitable! The Devil is indeed the ruler of this world; death and destruction are at work through unsaved humanity; even so, Satan's family of unbelievers are indeed his offspring and, therefore, instruments of death and destruction (John 14:30; 2 Corinthians 4:4)!

But Jesus is our Savior and Deliverer, and His Father is also our *Daddy*! He is calling all of His imagers to repentance. Jesus has the final say and not death nor the Devil! And He will have the last word regarding those who have become His *Daddy's* children! And also, regarding those who will suffer with their daddy, the Devil for all time (Matthew 3:2; Luke 5:32; Revelation 20:11-15)!

Where there is abuse within what should be the most sacred space and secure place for a child – their home and in the safety of the arms of Dad. When a child in particular or an individual doesn't feel safe at home, they may not likely feel safe anywhere because their trust and security have been lost due to betrayal. Now, for a moment, consider the latent stress that such a one is constantly under; is there any wonder why many are dealing with mental or, better yet, spiritual health crises. Countless youth have experienced horrific abuse from men (males) whose care they were under! And it is not uncommon for a child who has been in this way violated to become gravely psychologically affected; herein, Satan's prime objective is accomplished.

I've heard reports, and perhaps you have also, from young people and adults who experienced said abuse. They share how the abuse negatively affected them or still affects them, even to the degree of some not rightly viewing their sexual identity and or being confused about proper sexual behavior or orientation. Damn, Dads!... what a dilemma you have created because you are not in your right mind and right place under your Creator's loving authority.

Men, because you are reading this book, your Creator and my *Daddy* now has your attention. He is present to help you to become godly men, husbands, and dads. ***Simply surrender yourself over to the Watchful and Loving Care of Jesus.*** In doing so, He will begin a work in you that perhaps you have not been able to imagine! God will give you a new name and a new identity... He longs to call you – son!

Perhaps you now better understand why I hold this matter of misandry and *Disdain for Daddy and Hatred of Men* as being of greater concern and significance than the matter of misogyny. However, this is not to downplay the issue of misogyny where it is evident. But now I will remind you of what I expressed in both my preface and introduction to this book: *"For Satan to get* (render ineffective, subdue, or murder) *the man of the house, he, therefore, gets the house,"* meaning all under Daddy's care. It is for this reason God needs godly men and dads who will stand united with Him as Difference Makers so that we may protect His homes and the women and children who have been entrusted to our care. You do know?... Satan is also gunning for them!

The Seed Battle

I will now address the matter from Scripture that further drives home my position and the reason for the Daddy Dilemma, coupled with this disdain and hatred that many have against men. In Genesis chapter 3:15, we find the following text: "And I will put enmity between you and the woman, and between your offspring (or *seed*, KJV) and hers. He will crush your head, and you will strike his heel." This passage introduces the cosmic conflict that defines or shapes humanity's struggles against spiritual evil or wickedness that are seen unceasingly as manifesting or being played out on Earth.

In this historical text, we are provided God's initial prophetic battle cry and declaration of spiritual warfare! This unprecedented conflict will have as its battleground the earth. Throughout time as we know it, mankind will become either agents and true imagers unto God or His enemies, such rebellious ones who choose to remain under the *Banner of Sin and Death*, as agents and imitators of Satan, the *Great Deceiver* and god of this fallen world (2 Corinthians 4:4; John 8:44; Revelation 12:9).

Expounding upon this spiritual dilemma before us, the tension within this text and the imminent global conflict between the woman and Satan: This endless hostility, murderous, bloody conflict, and enmity that was unleashed and ignited that began at God's announced judgment has continued endlessly on earth between this woman or Eve's "offspring" and Satan's (or Devil's) "offspring."

What fallen humanity can't see and what Christians, seemingly, largely fail to with persistent spiritual discernment, keep within their thoughts. Is that this world's dilemmas and battles, which wrongly are often dealt with or fought solely in the flesh – mankind against their fellow man, as evidenced throughout creation's suffering and from unimaginable violence and emotional abuse; by the way, which often has as its instigator the malevolent satanic or demonic realm!

Therefore, we must be vigilant and mindful that our dilemmas and/or conflicts are, in fact, spiritual in essence – spiritual wickedness warring against us from without. However, it's primarily the spiritual conflict that we are more often confronted by from within each of us, resulting from our fallen or sinful human nature that wars against our renewed or *Born Again spirit* (Romans 7:18-25; Ephesians 6:10-18). As for those not *Regenerated*, this condition speaks for itself! Meanwhile, as children of God, our bodies await their redemption while we engage in spiritual battle to keep our flesh or corrupt bodies under subjection (Romans 8:23;1 Corinthians 9:27).

To counter *Man's* dilemmas, God in Genesis 3:15 also prophesies narrowing or bringing into focus His **Divine Difference Maker;** even so, our *Deliverer* and *Defender,* Jesus, who has and ultimately will bring an end to this global conflict or **Diabolical Dilemma** that mankind is faced with. A Hebrew word study of the rendering "offspring," when translated to its original Hebrew interpretation, is presented as the word **Seed or Zera**.

By rendering Eve's *offspring* as *seed,* this word is understood as a singular individual, which points to this one described as *he*. And this **Seed** or **He** who will crush Satan's head underscores the prophetic and spiritual nature of the text's discourse. The hostility or hatred that Eve would have against Satan and he against her, extending perpetually throughout their familial lineage, actually points to and culminates with Mary, the mother who, through *Divine* conception (the Holy Spirit) womb sheltered, protected, and nourished this **Seed**, entrusted to her care as none other than Jesus. It will be Jesus – the **Seed**, who will utterly destroy Satan and all who are allied with Him.

As prophesied in Genesis 3:15, Jesus is the promised child born of Mary (Isaiah 9:6) or the woman's *seed* according to biology or God's fleshly incarnation; this is Jesus – this **Seed** choosing to clothe Himself in flesh or taking on the form of *Man* (Philippians 2:6-8; Galatians 4:4,5). More importantly, Jesus is the sinless Son of God according to the Holy Spirit or the *Ruach HaKodosh* (Matthew 1:18-20; Luke 1:35; Romans 1:3,4). This **He** – the *Unique Promised* Son of God and second or final Adam (1 Corinthians 15:45-47) points back to Genesis 3:15, therein the first announcement of the good news, or Protoevangelium, heralding Jesus the Messiah and *Conquering King* who will ultimately crush Satan's head (John 1:49; Revelation 19:11-16)!

As shown, the Genesis 3 text highlights the historical enmity within mankind, including the *seed* of the woman – Jesus, who is the sinless, second or final Adam. According to Scripture, this enmity is with Satan and his offspring – fallen and rebellious humanity against the children of God. Clearly, this battle furthermore, points to the fallen angelic realm, reflecting the deeper spiritual battle that has shaped the course of human history and relationships, not excluding the challenges or dilemmas posed by ungodly fathers, men and boys lost in sin, or such persons who may also be under the influence of spiritual wickedness.

A Mother's Suffering - A Mother's Dilemma!

As Scripture has indicated, all godly women either have or will come to recognize that the dilemmas or suffering of their offspring, no matter how it manifests and against their sons, in particular, originates from sin and principally from the Devil himself. Because God designed males to be spiritual leaders, Satan specifically desires to keep in captivity sinful males, thereby rendering them ineffective imagers of God, if not destroy them! However, Satan's initial diabolical aim, as reported through the Biblical account, was to abort or kill the promised *Child/Seed* as provided within the Genesis narrative and as seen throughout Israel's earliest history. This meant that Satan specifically targeted all male children conceived by or born of Hebrew or Jewish women who had Yahweh as their God (Exodus 1:15-22; Esther 3:8-13; Matthew 2:16-18).

That said, the Devil desires ferociously to exterminate all male children if it were only possible or, at the very least, to render them or keep them as ineffective imagers of God. The Devil is keenly aware of the male's potential, in that boys might be brought up or raised to reverence God, their Creator, thereby becoming Satan's fierce enemies as *Mighty Men of God.* And as such, protectors and spiritual leaders of their dominions – their sacred spaces, families, and all under their care! Such godly men and *Dads as Difference Makers,* thereby becoming a direct threat to Satan's plan to destroy godly families, hence, a dilemma for Satan. Men, this is the only dilemma that we should readily embrace!

What must be understood is that men and boys rightly orientated or becoming sons of God are more so a threat to Satan's agenda and schemes of familial destruction than women. Yes, *"For Satan to get the man of the house, he gets the house,"* or those who are under the male's care. Satan vehemently opposes God's design and purpose for family and His representatives here on earth. Therefore, men and you women who are raising boys, Satan desires nothing more than to take them out or render male imagers of God useless!

We are told in Luke's gospel, regarding the woman, Mary, the mother of Jesus, as a result of this gift and blessing of a child, nevertheless because of Him – the *Unique Son of God,* "That a sword will pierce her soul." These prophetic words were foreshadowing or pointing to the satanic malicious and ill-treatment of Jesus instigated by none other than Satan. Yet this was Jesus giving of Himself, His self-sacrifice, over to the torturous and brutal murder He endured at the hands of Satan's children. Even so, this was Jesus' purposed and appointed assignment, to meet with humiliation and crucifixion so that He may address *Man's* dilemmas and confront death and the Devil (John 6:38 & 10: 17,18; Isaiah 53:3-7; Matthew 27:27-44; Hebrew 2:14,15 & 12:2; 1 Peter 2:23; John 8:34-36).

At the time of this prophetic announcement, Mary could only behold Jesus – *Emanuel, God with us* (Matt. 1:22,23), as merely her own son and baby – flesh of her flesh. But some *33 years* later, she would witness the ultimate cruelty that her son would have to undergo because of the satanic and demonic forces of evil – hence the sword piercing Mary's soul! It would be only after Jesus' resurrection from death and the grave that she would fully come to know her child as the *Very Preexistent Son of God* (Luke 1:26-35; Luke 2:22-35)!

Mary's anxiety from the announcement of the sword that would pierce her soul, although she could not comprehend the magnitude of the painful future or predetermined dilemmas that awaited her and her child, was set in motion when she agreed to conceive the *Son of God*, through the Holy Spirit (Luke 1:38). As clearly portrayed in the life of Mary, living for God can present us with unique trials in addition to those challenges and dilemmas we will encounter because we live in a fallen world.

Scripture does not provide us the thoughts that may have been racing through Mary's mind nor her mental state when she realized that she had actually become pregnant through *Supernatural or Divine* means. If you are able, mentally put yourself in her place: can you begin to imagine what her thoughts may have been as she pondered the ominous prophetic message spoken to her by Simeon (Luke 2:25-35). And, from what she had to process that was spoken to her by the angel Gabriel and Elizabeth (Luke:1:26-38 & 39-45).

This was quite a bit of revelation or information she had daily racing through her mind, and I would imagine nightly she wrestled with these revelations as she attempted to go to sleep. Imagine all the unknowns she possibly pondered and restless thoughts from each day as her feet hit the floor at Dawn's rising even while she raced after the cares and concerns of that day! Not to mention the thoughts she entertained regarding Joseph, her fiancé, who was now faced with an unfathomable dilemma himself... His pregnant wife-to-be and the child she carried that wasn't his!

The point of the sword, no doubt, could be felt as Mary's unanswered questions and the uncertainty of her future began to press upon her soul. I am sure that with the passing of time, when Mary heard and witnessed that her own people were beginning to turn against her son, this piercing of her soul was, therefore, ever-present! I imagine she pondered the actual meaning of the words spoken to her regarding her son, as she was also told *he would be great and accomplish mighty things!* However, this would be at a great cost of suffering to them both, leaving her distressed of heart and a piercing of her soul, even so, a piercing of the side of her son, Jesus (John 19:34)!

However, I remind you that these dilemmas that Mary and Jesus encountered were preordained by God. Even so, Jesus also prepares and forewarns us. He says to His Father's children... "In the world, you will have tribulation, but be of good cheer, I have overcome the world (John 16:33, NKJV). Here in this text, Jesus wants us to plainly understand that in this fallen world, tribulations are inevitable. Or, as I have provided in my rephrasing, Jesus could have very well stated, "In this fallen world, you will face dilemmas of all sorts. Nevertheless, I am your *Deliverer and Difference Maker* that will enable you to overcome your dilemmas and this evil world. Therefore, be confident and courageous in and through me!

As for Mary, having had it stated to her that her son Jesus would be great and accomplish wonderful things, coupled with the suffering that they would have to endure, certainly did not make any sense in her natural reasoning. Suffering never makes sense, and certainly to those who, in their thinking, have done no wrong! However confounding the matter all the more, this suffering, along with her blessing of the child from the Holy Spirit, was God's prophetic words which had been spoken unto her; this is what heightens Mary's tension. Mary and the Jewish people were anticipating their *Messianic Deliverer and Difference Maker*, but this aspect of her specific suffering she could not reconcile with.

As it was with her and often with those of us who are parents, she saw these threats and attacks against her son that, as a mother, she could not distance herself from; his pain and suffering became hers! And naturally, His enemies also became her enemies, however, in the natural or physical sense. As it were, the enmity between her and her *Seed* – Jesus (Yeshua) with Satan had come to bear. However, Mary could not comprehend the spiritual significance and warfare that was before she and her son. The very hand of Satan would be set against Jesus and her by the hands of spiritually broken people who belonged to the Devil. And, therefore, subsequently influenced as his agents, even so, they being one with their Daddy – the Devil (John 8:44).

Mary, as with those of us who are children of God, may feel from time to time when opposed or experiencing conflict; in the heat of the moment, we can only see what is taking place before us, or we reason with our worldly mindset. Therefore, we have the tendency because we still retain mortal or flawed bodily compositions to react or respond from the flesh or natural reasoning; this we must prayerfully guard ourselves against.

Unlike Mary, during this point in her life, we who are children of God have been informed from Scripture that we are not fighting against flesh and blood – other imagers of God. But rather against spiritual wickedness. Therefore, we are not to see a presumed "enemy" or imager of God as our actual enemy. We must maintain, through our spiritual enlightenment, that there is more going on behind the scenes or in the unseen spiritual realm than what meets our eyes (Ephesians 6:12).

Resulting from these troubling dilemmas that were encountered by Mary and her son, her grief was inextricably and biologically united with him. Consequently, from their troublings, but from her mindset alone and natural understanding, his enemies most assuredly became her enemies. From her fleshly worldview of the battles with His enemies, even as they hung and tortured her son upon the cross, I will posit that Mary was also traumatized by all that she heard and witnessed... But of course, she had to be! This is what evil does; this is what Satan wants, "to kill and destroy" God's imagers! But God sustains those who He calls, and His grace and mercy, for a duration of His choosing, are experienced by all! But trouble will not last always!

It is within reason to believe that Mary either heard or witnessed the false accusations made against her beloved son. Mary had to have known about the plots of her people to have her child killed! Although Satan accomplished his mission – to strike or bruise Jesus' heel, he ultimately lost the battle; Jesus' foot is currently on the head of Satan, and the crushing of his head is imminent!

It was Mary's love for her grown baby, Jesus, that would compel her to observe the humiliation of the bloody and brutal murder and crucifixion of her promised son! This act of satanic wickedness against her child according to the flesh and the *Unique Son of God,* according to the Spirit, was the decisive piercing of Mary's soul! Nevertheless, this conflict was her son's to fight or patiently suffer alone in the flesh, and not hers. Neither could she nor anyone else, for that matter, withstand these spiritual forces of evil so that God's mission would be accomplished. Which was, and is, for Jesus, our *Deliverer and Difference Maker,* to ultimately deal with the *Daddy Dilemma* – the Devil himself.

And subsequently, for Jesus, our *Difference Maker,* to confront and deal with mankind's dilemmas through the giving or Self-sacrifice of Himself. Because some either are, and all were, at one point in time, the Devil's sons and daughters. Therefore, because of the *Devil-dilemma*, sin or corruption yet remains in our natural bodies, a dilemma that we as children of God must constantly war against (Romans 7:15-25; Galatians 5:16,17; 1 Peter 2:11)!

Thus, this cosmic battle against evil was foreknown and hence ordained by our *Daddy* (Acts 2:23; 1 Peter 1:19,20), therefore setting the stage for this supernatural confrontation that would take place between the *seed* of Mary according to the flesh and yet our *Daddy's Unique Son* according to His intrinsic Deity as Spirit or Elohim (the Hypostatic Union of Jesus or the *God-man* is once again in view).

These spiritual powers of **Light** and darkness figuratively squared off at the cross: mano a mano, **The Man of God**, and Satan. Although he – Satan was at work through his wicked children, assailed the God-man, Yeshua, in the flesh. Nevertheless, they did not win the ultimate battle, which is always spiritual in nature (John 1:5). Because *Man,* in essence, are also created spiritual beings or elohim, in the likeness of our *Daddy* and Creator, the *Sovereign Elohim*, our warfare is one with our Creator and *Daddy...* it is always spiritual in nature (John 4:24; Romans 1:20; Colossians 1:15).

However, unlike the imperceivable spiritual realm, externally, mankind's visible bodily glory or clothing is that of flesh, its origin from the earth, of which both have become corrupt because of sin and/or Satan. Resulting from mankind's inherent physical corruption and subsequent spiritual blindness, we act wrongly and also wrongly respond to conflict in the flesh – we respond with violence, harsh words, and wrong thinking. These are dilemmas that we must battle against and overcome.

The child of God must withstand such inclinations or temptations by exercising spiritual disciplines to withstand conflicts and evil that wars against us. We must bear in mind that our challenges of whatever sort, at the root, are spiritual, and therefore, we must resist carnal responses and confrontations that are futile when trying to address or confront that which is spiritual in nature. When we as children of God do this well or deal with challenges righteously, we become *Difference Makers* in the likeness of our *Daddy* (Hebrews 2:14,15; Romans; 16:20; Ephesians 6:12 and Job 10:11; 1 Corinthians 15:37-40; 2 Corinthians 5:1-4).

Satan's Miscalculation

Satan, who is designated a "strong man" in Matthew 12:29, as described as such, in his arrogance and pride, also attempted to overcome the second or final Adam, Yeshua – **The Mighty God-Man** *or* **Son of God** by overcoming Him bodily (Isaiah 9:6, Colossians 2:9; Matt. 28:18).

This confrontation between these two spirit beings (elohim), with Jesus being the **Ultimate Eternal Elohim,** the **God** *of gods* and the **Creator** of all angels (elohim), including the Cherub Lucifer, aka Satan – in his fallen state and other lesser gods (elohim) or rebellious spirits (Deuteronomy 10:17; Colossians 2:9-15 Psalms 82:1,6-7), was another and the final battle initiated by Satan in his attempt to *get* or takeout Jesus the **Man** over God's house or kingdom that he may thwart *Their* plan.

Just as Satan overcame Adam and attempted to overcome Jesus at the onset of His ministry while in the wilderness (Luke 4:1-13). This time, Satan, meeting Jesus at the cross, wrongly thought that he had triumphed over the **God-Man** at his crucifixion. However, Satan couldn't comprehend the Redemptive Plan of God, nor the spiritual significance of the self-sacrifice of the Son of God that would ultimately lead to Satan's decisive destruction or eternal end within the Gehenna or Lake of Fire (Matthew 25:41; Revelation 20:10)! What a miscalculation of the forces of evil!

1 Corinthians 2:7 tells us, *"No, we declare God's wisdom, a mystery that has been hidden and that God destined for our glory before time began. 8 None of the **rulers** of this age understood it, for if they had, they **would not have** crucified the Lord of glory."* In **Colossians 2:15**, we are told that Jesus, *having disarmed the powers and authorities, he made a public spectacle of them, triumphing over them by the cross.*

I will now point out a matter I've determined to be significant regarding these two spirit beings: The rendering of the Hebrew word elohim describing Jesus and Satan is a masculine plural translation of elohim in the context provided. The Devil, who is also designated as the father (linguistically masculine) of all who practice wickedness and who reject Jesus, saw his chance after several millenniums had passed to finally murder the *Promised Seed* of Genesis 3:15 now that He had been clearly identified (Luke 3:21,22 and 4:1-13).

Although angels or elohim are not described by gender. However, with the rendering of the masculine usage of elohim, additionally, according to Scripture, men being God's ordained leaders of their home and His commanders and warriors during battle. I further posit that Satan's primary aim is to target males for destruction, though he is not a respecter of persons when it comes to rendering people ineffective or bringing them to ruin!

This male child – Jesus was He – the **Seed** of the Woman who had been prophetically commissioned to crush Satan's head. Satan, having mustered all of the essential ruling powers of Jesus' time, those who were, in fact, influenced and beguiled by Satan and the forces of evil rallied against the **God-Man** in what they thought was a triumphal procession. They, therefore, led Jesus to the cross on Calvary's Hill to be tortured or crucified. The "strongman," Satan, veiled from the eyes of his accomplices in the murder of the **God-Man** – Jesus, most assuredly proudly stood watch and paraded himself in victory when he saw Jesus' head slump as He gave up His last breath while hanging from the cross (Matthew 27:50).

In Satan's misguided and constrained reasoning and understanding, *Death* or even Satan himself had defeated his nemesis and **Dilemma**, the **Seed** of the Woman. But in truth, Jesus' self-sacrifice was a decisive victory that He – the Son of God according to the Spirit won when He overcame the cross, *Death*, and the grave through His bodily resurrection! The woman's **Seed**, this suffering Jesus endured, His self-sacrifice, and seemingly defeat was His heel being struck as prophesied in Genesis 3:15 (Matthew 26:50-54; Hebrews 2:14,15; Colossians 2:15; Revelation 1:18).

Satan clearly understood that for him to *get* (render ineffective, subdue, or murder) the **God-Man** or the **Man of God** appointed over His *Daddy's* house. Like Satan *got* Adam, overcame his house, voided out God's expectations for him, and usurped Adam's authority, Satan wrongly thought that he would also *get* God's house or His kingdom if he were to *get* the **Man** – Jesus, who was appointed over His Father's house.

Mona a Mona, Satan once again came against God's appointed **Man,** even so the *seed* of the Woman. But this time, it would not be so that Satan would overcome God's **Man** and His *Unique Son!* Jesus' seemingly defeat and burial would be the very course prophesied and purposed by our *Daddy*. That Jesus may conquer death and the grave and reign as Victor over the Devil Dilemma, as our **Deliverer** and **Difference Maker** (Isaiah Chapter 53; Psalm Chapter 22; 2 Corinthians 2:8; Ephesians 1:3-14)!

As for Mary, even though she felt the pain of spiritual warfare and the agony of what felt like and she believed to be utter defeat! Just the same, this spiritual battle that her *Child* was engaged in was not hers. But rather, His decisive battle for *her*! And not just her, but all who are forced to deal with, struggle, and fight against the *Devil Dilemma*! Mary's traumatic suffering over her child's murder was excruciating, but it was not her pain and momentary loss to endure alone (John 19:26; Galatians 5:14 and 6:2).

Together, We are To Faithfully Endure Hardship

As children of God and His family of *Believers*, we are commanded to care for one another, to rejoice with one another, and even to grieve with those who are in sorrow (Romans 12:15; Hebrews 10:24,25). In the wicked and uncertain days of this world, which are before God's sons and daughters. It is extremely important that we, as men of God, learn to bond together so that we may encourage and strengthen one another through Christ.

The challenges or spiritual battles we as Christians face are ultimately the Lord's (2 Chronicles 20:15)! Yet together as children of God, we faithfully endure our hardships and these challenges, in or through the Lord, and engage in spiritual warfare with Jesus, our *Deliverer,* and *Defender* against spiritual evil (Ephesians 6:10-18; 2 Corinthians 10:3-5)!

Jesus, as His *Daddy's Perfect Imager* and *Representative* on earth, accomplished what the first man, Adam, failed to accomplish – to protect his house and dominion given to him by God to steward. Jesus, our **Difference Maker**, became like unto man, the *Final* and *Sinless Adam*, that He may *Man up* as the selfless **God-man** and **Servant King.** Jesus came to earth to do battle against the spiritual forces of evil that oppose you and me! He came to His *Daddy's* lost children, even so, the children of *Their* making! Not only did Jesus honor His *Abba* and protect His Father's house, but now we are one with our *Daddy* to safely dwell for all time in our Father's Kingdom – the New Heaven and New Earth that is soon to come!

Men of God, you who are called to be *Difference Makers.* Concerning this extremely wicked generation before us, we must also man up and strap up, armed with God's Word of Truth! We must recognize that we are engaged in all-out spiritual warfare and, therefore, stay prayed up in the power of the Holy Spirit; we must! We must understand that these evil forces of the unseen realm, which have been opposing us since our conception, not only desire to take us out as our Father's leaders and warriors who are built to be protectors and defenders. But these maleficent forces of evil also seek to destroy our marriages and children that have been entrusted to our care by God!

As godly men, we are our *Daddy's* first and foremost line of defense for those in our care or under our influence! However, we must be mindful that we are not warring against other imagers of God – our lost brothers and sisters. Instead, we are to engage in spiritual warfare through the spiritual disciplines of prayer, arming ourselves with the Word of God and the shield of faith – which is our assurance in Jesus, who is our eternal Hope! Furthermore, through our acts of service, we are to demonstrate love and self-sacrifice to and before others so that our lost brothers and sisters may be won over to Christ... This is spiritual warfare; this is mission and ministry accomplished!

My brothers, we desperately need to see the urgency to reorientate our thinking or align our way of living with our *Daddy* so that He may teach us how to become *Difference Makers* after His likeness! It is only when we become one with our *Father* and purpose in our hearts or minds that we want to be like our *Daddy* that we, with the help of the Holy Spirit, begin to develop into godly men, men who know how to look after their spiritual welfare, others, and, especially, those whom our Father has entrusted to our care and spiritual leadership!

On the other hand, men who choose to remain one with this world or the Devil, your daddy. Look, I remind you yet again, no matter the "good" that you may seem to do, and certainly when you fail to render godly guidance and to lead your offspring to **Daddy the Difference Maker – Jesus himself**... you have failed them! Now taking into account, if you have brought harm and trauma to your child[ren] in the likes of what's been previously mentioned, you've certainly damned or cursed your offspring! Now, resulting from their disdain and hatred of you, how can you be surprised when they one day exclaim, *Damn Daddy,* or some other profane words to express their hurt and hatred toward you! Instead of displaying love for you as Daddy, the Difference Maker as purposed by God. They can only see you as Daddy, their Dilemma!

CHAPTER 4

Damned and Damn Daddy!

As a young man in my early twenties, I, too, had known hatred and disdain for my dad. Even so, periodic moments of feeling tremendous loss, loneliness, the sense of inadequacy, hurt, anger, and disappointment resulting from their failure to show up, be present, and be godly men…You heard it right, *their* failure! I'll elaborate on this matter soon enough. However, before doing so, I will acknowledge giving thought to these men who, in various and even unidentifiable ways, helped to shape in some way the good, the bad, and the ugly of my life's story.

Consequently, because of their gross failure or as Daddy Dilemmas, I too can identify and certainly empathize with those who shout profanity towards their dads and who exclaim, as expressed by the young lady in the previous chapter, "I hate my daddy!" Or others who cry out with visceral pain within their souls…Damn, Daddy!

In spite of my personal Daddy Dilemmas, I will contribute just these three things to having kept me somewhat centered or grounded and from becoming excessively detrimental to myself and others during my most vulnerable years:

1. My positive and considerate mental disposition.

2. A prayerfully loving yet stern and firm mother when it came to my conduct.

3. And not the least of which, the grace of God… even so, my Mother's *Daddy,* whom she learned to trust as a child.

My mother informed me later in my life that she did a lot of praying and that she continues to do so. My mother was my Difference Maker, and for this, I am grateful! I praise my *Daddy* for a praying and loving mother – Joyce, and for Him inclining His ear to her prayers. I'm able to write this book and others I've authored because of my mother's relationship with her *Daddy* and because of her, now mine.

From my experience regarding my personal Daddy Dilemmas, I've identified a few of my deficiencies, with none of them substantially impeding my youthful development, neither successfully working against my forward progression and positive outlook on life, nor how I viewed or currently view myself, or how others saw and see me. The road was not easy, and I had my questionable and uncertain moments. Nevertheless, I can say that I fared well. Thanks be to God, my *Daddy the Difference Maker*!

However, statistical data, as well as empirical data, indicate that for many youth and adults whose life experiences are similar to mine, their outcomes are not always as favorable in light of my life's journey. Certainly, where one's upbringing and environment consist of or are met with greater challenges, the more difficult their journey. Some are able to escape their life's trappings or dilemmas, while many others remain stuck in their situation, haunted and/or cursed because of their *Damned and Damn* Daddy!

Working as a Police Officer for nearly three decades, with three of those years being worked in a middle school, I saw and encountered numerous situations where kids were negatively affected by the Daddy Dilemma or from being raised in dysfunctional homes. When parents were not around within the community's microcosm of the school, a child's poor conduct and emotional state becoming apparent when their parents weren't present often indicated that things were not well at their homes. However, there were times when kids showed out in front of their parent[s] or, because of their parent, this was often the case with a parent who lacked basic parental skills.

Unfortunately, in today's society, we see our youth behaving badly or inappropriately almost anywhere and at any time! However, where a godly or even a good dad is functioning in their rightful station, rarely is this the case. Tragically, it's uncommon these days to see dads operating in their right station as godly leaders over their families. From the number of stories that could possibly be shared, here are three stories with one contrasting narrative I recall regarding *Dad the Difference Makers* and *Dad the Dilemma.*

Dad, the Difference Maker

While sitting outside on what is known as "The Main Street" at Southpoint Mall in my hometown of Durham, N.C. A dad and mom of African descent had sat at a table beside Barnes and Noble, approximately 30 yards across from me. The dad and I simply acknowledged and came into what I will describe as coming to an agreement with one another by simply making eye contact and a slight head nod… this is a man thing!

Situated between us was a large, somewhat rounded sculpture containing a small water spout and a pool of water with large art décor inside and outside of the small pool. As the parents sat talking, the dad allowed his daughter, who was no more than perhaps five years of age, to play around the sculpture. It was apparent to me that the child was well-behaved and that she played under her father's watchful, protective, and loving eye as she was guided by whatever instructions he had provided to his little princess. This innocent little girl and gift from God didn't have a care in the world because she had a dad who was her Difference Maker!

I watched her playfulness and this beautiful family dynamic with a slight smile on my face and a huge smile inwardly! However, as the child played, she ventured into a blind spot caused by a large column that prevented the Father's view of his daughter. The dad lovingly called out to his child, and she obediently came back into his view. However, she was unaware that her daddy had temporarily lost sight of her.

With the child's enjoyment and excitement caused by the sculptures and water, once again, she momentarily ventured from her protective and loving Father's sight. Me now looking in the child's daddy's direction, with his eyes momentarily connecting with mine. I don't know exactly what body language I presented to this Father, perhaps another head nod, but my thought was, "Brother, I have my eyes on your daughter!" We exchanged no words; however, we were on the same page regarding his daughter now also being under the watchful care and the trusted eye of another man – me, a Difference Maker.

The remainder of the time that he and his wife sat there talking because he had entrusted his daughter to me, he no longer showed concern when his daughter ventured from his sight. No doubt this child knew the love of her Daddy! However, from this beautiful family dynamic, I was able to experience this brother's love for his daughter and also this Difference Maker from afar. For this – his trust in me, I was overwhelmed and grateful to my brother for entrusting me to keep an eye on his precious daughter.

When he was about to depart with his lovely wife and daughter, once again, we briefly connected visually. With his non-verbal communication – a look and a nod, he responded, "I appreciate you!" The actions of a Father speak far louder and more profoundly than any words towards his offspring. This child, as she innocently and gleefully played and explored her surroundings, knew that her daddy loved her. And I knew that he loved her by his and her interactions, even so, the peaceful demeanor that I discern within his wife! As they walked away, he held his daughter's hand in his with his wife by his side. This moment has been retained in my memory primarily because I seldom see a distinguished African American couple outside of my sons demonstrate such a beautiful and loving family dynamic.

Here's another such story that's fitting as one that can be referred to as Dad the Difference Maker. It was near to two decades – on a Friday night at Hillside High School, Durham, NC, where Desmond played football. The stadium buzzed with the typical energy of a pre-game football crowd. Hundreds of fans filled the stands, their chatter and cheers creating a symphony of anticipation. Down on the sideline stood a dad, affectionately known by his nickname, *Coach Runt,* aka Antonio King. He was intently focused, preparing his team for the game that was just moments from starting. His wife and their newborn child – no more than a year old – were seated nearby in the stands with me.

Amid the noise and excitement, a sound pierced through the clamor: the unmistakable cry of his baby girl. What happened next left me amazed. Despite the chaos, Coach Runt heard her *single* cry. From his position on the sideline, nearly forty yards away, surrounded by the roaring crowd, his ears tuned instinctively to his child's cry. Immediately, he turned in the direction of his wife and daughter. For a moment, his attention left the game to ensure they were okay.

Seeing that all was well, he resumed his focus on preparing his players for the upcoming kickoff. That small yet powerful moment has stayed with me ever since. It showed me that Coach Runt wasn't just a coach or a father – he was the kind of dad who was attentive to his family's needs – hence Dad, a Difference Maker. His ability to respond, even amidst the noise and demands of life, is the hallmark of a true Difference Maker.

This moment reminds me of the likeness of God and how He responds to His children. Just as Coach Runt's ears were attuned to his daughter's cry despite the noise and distance, so God hears and recognizes the cries of His children, no matter how far or faint they may seem. God's care for us is constant and intentional. His attentiveness and readiness to respond demonstrate the ultimate example of what it means for God to be our **Omnipresent** and **Omniscient Difference Maker** (Psalm 139:7-10; Matthew 7:11; 1 Peter 3:12)!

Dad the Dilemma

As for the brief but profoundly contrasting story, I don't recall if I had previously met this child's dad or ever laid eyes on him. However, the mother of this child, her younger sister, and I attended the same church; we'd had some measure of interactions. My sons during this time were around the ages of these two princesses. Regarding the next occurrence or the Daddy Dilemma, the experience unfolded at church during a time of prayer. Unlike the children in the previous stories, this child felt abandoned and unloved by her dad. Had she ever known the love of her dad? Had she played under her father's watchful, protective, and loving eyes? Did she feel safe in her daddy's presence? To these questions, I don't have an answer.

We were attending Sunday service; however, now closing out the worship service with corporate prayer. Several church members had made their way to the altar to pray and submit prayer requests. This time together was always solemn, and, at times, it could become quite emotional. This day would be such a day! Prayer requests had been made... I seem to recall our time of prayer for many was coming to a tearful close. Then, an eruption of visceral emotions – a cry burst forth from the oldest child as she knelt on the floor, embraced by her mother and one or two others.

The pain could be felt in her voice, and everyone heard this child cry forth in tremendous anguish, "Why don't my daddy love me?!" "Why doesn't he love me?!" Recalling that moment, I now feel the tears swelling in my eyes as I felt and still feel that child's desperation and her inability to comprehend why her daddy didn't love her and why he wasn't there for her! This child's Daddy Dilemma was heard by everyone present, and her deep pain was experienced by many.

Here, we have the tell of three stories but with significant and life-changing consequences or outcomes. However, and with sadness of heart. I am inclined to believe that there are more similar stories and children who can relate to the latter situation than the first two loving family structures. Close to three decades ago, I remember hearing a song by the great street prophet, poet, lyrical genius, and storyteller Tupac Shakur. A ballad of his, or "Conscious Rap," struck a cord in my soul!

A Word From the Street Prophet Tupac Shakur

Tupac's passionate and well-crafted words, along with his unique vocal sound or intonation, like a magnet, pulled me into his mental space of internal spiritual conflict and pain! His Mama Drama and Daddy Dilemma resounded throughout his sermon presented in song. I'd never heard such language and heartfelt expression put into a rap track. Although his story and life were quite different than mine, nonetheless, his life was relatable, and I was able to feel his pain and struggle... Yes, I could empathize with my broken and spiritually challenged brother as he was trying to make sense of life's dilemmas and his Mama Drama because of his Daddy Dilemma.

As I continued to listen to Pac, he brought me to a point in his lyrical melodic story where he poignantly expressed, "No love from my daddy..." What a dilemma and crisis that he and far too many have had to endure and try to make sense of. Pac, in one sense, was also crying out, "Damn, Daddy! Daddy, why don't you love me?! Why don't you care?!"

Now, I want you to hear Tupac's continued lament throughout his following lyrical expression. Perhaps you may be able to relate; if not, perhaps you may be able to at least empathize with his emotional state. Pac's soul conflict and the pain resulting from his Daddy Dilemma were surely, in large part, the reason behind many of his poor choices. And, no doubt, that of countless others, both the young and the old, where there is "No love from daddy" and subsequently no love for one's daddy because he did not man up or wasn't there for you.

"Dear Mama"

"You are appreciated.
When I was young, me and my mama had beef.
17 years old, kicked out on the streets
Though back at the time, I never thought I'd see her face.
Ain't a woman alive that could take my mama's place
Suspended from school
And scared to go home, I was a fool.
With the big boys breaking all the rules
I shed tears with my baby sister over the years.
We was poorer than the other little kids.
And even though we had different daddies, the same drama
When things went wrong, we'd blame mama.
I reminisce on the stress I caused; it was hell.
Huggin' on my mama from a jail cell
And who'd think in elementary, hey
I'd see the penitentiary one day?
And running from the police, that's right.
Mama catch me, put a whoopin' to my backside.
And even as a crack fiend, mama
You always was a black queen, mama.
I finally understand
For a woman, it ain't easy trying to raise a man.
You always was committed.
A poor single mother on welfare, tell me how you did it.
There's no way I can pay you back, but the plan.
Is to show you that I understand; you are appreciated.

[Reggie Green and "Sweet Franklin" (2Pac):]
Lady, don't you know we love ya? (Dear Mama)
Sweet lady, place no one above ya (You are appreciated)
Sweet lady, don't you know we love ya?

[2pac:]
Now, ain't nobody tell us it was fair
No love from my daddy, 'cause the coward wasn't there
He passed away, and I didn't cry 'cause my anger.
wouldn't let me feel for a stranger
They say I'm wrong, and I'm heartless, but all along.
I was looking for a father; he was gone.
I hung around with the thugs.
And even though they sold drugs
They showed a young brother love.
I moved out and started really hangin'.
I needed money of my own, so I started slangin'.
I ain't guilty 'cause even though I sell rocks.
It feels good putting money in your mailbox.
I love paying rent when the rent is due.
I hope you got the diamond necklace that I sent to you.
'Cause when I was low, you was there for me
And never left me alone because you cared for me.
And I could see you coming home after work late.
You're in the kitchen, trying to fix us a hot plate.
You just working with the scraps you was given.
And Mama made miracles every Thanksgivin'.
But now the road got rough, you're alone.
You're trying to raise two bad kids on your own
And there's no way I can pay you back, but my plan
Is to show you that I understand; you are appreciated.

[Reggie Green and "Sweet Franklin" (2Pac):]
Lady, don't you know we love ya? (Dear Mama)
Sweet lady, place no one above ya (You are appreciated)
Sweet lady, don't you know we love ya?

[2pac:]
Pour out some liquor, and I reminisce.
'Cause through the drama, I can always depend on my mama
And when it seems that I'm hopeless
You say the words that can get me back in focus.
When I was sick as a little kid
To keep me happy, there's no limit to the things you did
And all my childhood memories
Are full of all the sweet things you did for me
And even though I act crazy
I gotta thank the Lord that you made me.
There are no words that can express how I feel.
You never kept a secret, always stayed real.
And I appreciate how you raised me
And all the extra love that you gave me
I wish I could take the pain away.
If you can make it through the night, there's a brighter day.
Everything will be alright if you hold on.
It's a struggle every day; gotta roll on.
And there's no way I can pay you back, but my plan.
Is to show you that I understand; you are appreciated.

[Reggie Green and Sweet Franklin (2Pac):]
Lady, don't you know we love ya? (Dear Mama)
Sweet lady, place no one above ya (You are appreciated)
Sweet lady, don't you know we love ya? (Dear Mama)

> Sweet lady
> Lady (Dear Mama)
> Lady
> Lady"

There is much that can be analyzed from Tupac's words, which, I am certain, has been done from Barbershop talk to institutions of higher learning. As it was with Pac's situation, and as I've demonstrated, a lot of finger-pointing has been directed at Dads. And I will maintain and emphasize that this is rightly so. However, lest we forget, we all, who are now children of God, were sinfully broken or born with a sinful nature, and without our *Spiritual Daddy's* equipping and regeneration of our destitute souls, many remain desperately lost and struggling in their spiritual brokenness or even deadness (Psalm 51:5 & 58:3; Romans 5:12).

Just the same and in varying measures, each of us who are one with Jesus has something – some sin-struggle that we wrestle against, occasionally if not persistently. And if we are honest, there are times we, who are born-again *Believers* in Christ, are found on the losing end of a particular sin or spiritual skirmish. We, therefore, must also take into consideration these struggling men and dads. Up to this point, no direct attention has been given to the Daddy Dilemmas and/or the trauma that many men or daddies have also experienced growing up, therefore leading to their shortcomings, failures, and their inability to commit to, care for, and to lead those who are supposed to be under their stewardship and protection.

Now, to once again quote brother Tupac, however, with a slight modification, "*No love from dads cause the cowards weren't there.*" Truth be told, there are weak and irresponsible men who have run from their manly obligations as dads and husbands – hence, they are cowards. Whether they are considered cowards or described in some other negative descriptives, their sinfulness or being godless individuals, or failures as responsible dads or husbands didn't happen in a vacuum. Cause-and-effect – having godly dads or not, good versus evil, and sin that resides within each of us are perpetually at work in and around us all. And as I believe and have shared already, satanic evil is against boys and men in particular!

More often than not, dysfunction within a home, whether with or without dads or husbands, is often preceded by a pattern or the example of *gone* or ungodly Dads. Godly Dads *missing in action* (MIA) is the common denominator with the widespread Daddy Dilemma facing grown men, which will include their sons and daughters, the next generation of affected adults unless there is a reversal or reorientation of themselves with my *Daddy* and God our *Difference Maker*! What we are seeing is that these failures of men are merely images of their dads. Or their dads being their dilemmas because they could not or did not adequately train their sons on how to become godly men.

Only proper orientation with our God and Creator is where fallen mankind's solution or fix resides. Until such orientation or oneness is restored through spiritual regeneration within broken men and mankind with the *Divine Difference Maker,* these foreshadowing Daddy Dilemmas or merely biological seed donors will continue to thoughtlessly plant their corrupt seed and impregnate these hopefully misguided and, too, hopelessly spiritually broken and desperate women; women longing for companionship or a husband, and in turn, without considering the consequences, they lay with these mere corrupt seed donors, conceive and give birth to their child, resulting from a fleeting moment of hopeful pleasure from a man who is spiritually ill-equipped to attend to you; nor y'all's child!

Missing In Action - Missing After Action

Because of each of your thoughtless choices to engage in a moment of otherwise meaningless sexual gratification, your child will be met with challenges that affect every aspect of his or her being. Additionally, the challenges of being raised by a single mother who will embody *Mama Drama* because of the *Daddy Dilemma*! Everyone will be negatively affected, and perhaps for generations to come, because of a moment of hopeful sexual expression for the woman; as for the man, simply added seconds for sexual gratification. I will now repeat a rather damning comment that I made in my previous book:

"What I am about to say here results from a boy's mind, aka that of an irresponsible man. This may be difficult for a single mother to hear and accept and perhaps even more so for a fatherless child. I believe the reason why some fathers leave their responsibility or never take responsibility or care for their child[ren] is: There was no love or care for the mother of their child. So, why would they love or care for a child conceived in the heat of thoughtless, self-gratifying passion and sin?"

"When a child is conceived through this kind of unholy union, the father feels little to no pressure or obligation to do right by the mother of his child, let alone the child. As a result, he can just abandon or never acknowledge his responsibility or child. Sex was all that was wanted from the female. A child was not a part of the plan! Having gotten what he wanted – sex; however, more than what he bargained for – a child, he now ghosts the situation or becomes **"MIA"** Missing In Action or perhaps better stated **"MAA"** Missing After Action! Daily, this tragic drama is played out time and time again... And who suffers the most – the fatherless child!"

One of the great tragedies facing mankind is the lack of consideration given to bringing a child into this world or the consequences of the misuse or abuse of sexual relations. In my previous book, *"Not What I Wanted, Nevertheless, Everything That I Needed,"* I extensively elaborate on the subjects of the misuse and abuse of sexual relations within these thoughts: **Sex Gone Wild** and **Sex Weaponized!** I'm inclined to believe more people give thought to where and how they spend their money or on things that really don't matter than they do in the case of having a child, if any thought is given at all during unbridled copulation.

It's Not About Perfection, Instead Getting it Right - In this, Daddy is Well Pleased

While raising my sons, there were certain moral values I had instilled within me and engrained within them. I was a godly Dad; however, I was yet maturing in my faith and spiritual understanding and, therefore, even an ongoing and necessary work in progress. During that time, I don't think that anyone could rightly negatively critique the way I parented or led my family. That doesn't mean everyone agreed with my approach or method of leading my home.

Parenting and leading my family considering my less-than-favorable upbringing, nevertheless, with the grace of God, the knowledge and wisdom that I did have working for me, my family turned out, as I see things, as being ideal or righteous, before my God. Under the circumstances regarding my upbringing, I am confident my *Daddy* looks upon the outcome of the Scott family and is well pleased!

Make no mistake about it; there is no perfect marriage, person, or family. However, where God is honored, and one's home or you are led by the

Holy Spirit, much can be done right or be viewed as righteous before God; in this, our *Daddy* is well pleased! As I continued to mature as a dad and husband, along the way and early in my marriage, I greatly erred; furthermore, I could have made better personal choices and offered better guidance for my family. In my first book, I presented an involved or detailed negative critique of myself as I shared my gross sinfulness! Therefore, in this book, I will not revisit my failures and shortcomings; they have been clearly stated!

I will say this: My actions brought about immense emotional hurt for my wife. However, in large part, because of her personality and I owning my failure as a husband, Mama Drama did not manifest. Although during my season of great folly, I had become a Dilemma, my wife didn't know about my wrongdoings until some ten years later, when I chose to disclose my failure as a husband. My sons were quite young when I acted as a Dilemma, but neither did my action at the time of my foolishness, which occurred almost a decade prior, affect them, my wife, or my home directly. Read my previous book if you haven't already. You will see spiritual warfare as the forces of evil came after me and my family. Satan was after me; he was hell-bent on getting me – *the man over God's house,* the house or family that my *Daddy* had entrusted to my care.

Now, as a mature (not perfected) and even a victorious man of God, I am keenly aware that I have much to offer others from the mistakes I have made, additionally from the battles I've won! And not the least of which, from what the Holy Spirit has taught me, resulting from the error of my ways as well as the impartation of His truth. Therefore, through my first book, additionally this book, and at other times, I provide counsel, knowledge, and wisdom to others when the opportunity is provided.

You Must Be a Better Dad

I am inclined to believe that my sons have certainly benefitted from my guidance. That said, in the past 3 decades, much has changed in the world – for the worst since they were innocent and typical boys in search of fun and laughter. The parenting days of my sons have long passed. However, there are times when I am compelled to share with them some concern or truth that I know they will benefit from. Here's one such concern and truth that are interwoven.

Before, they were dads, and after they became fathers, I said to them individually, "You must be a better Dad than me as you raise your children. Take them to church and have them participate in the life of the church. However, they can't simply be religious – that is, merely faithful to church work or participation. Your children, at an early age, must come to know for themselves Jesus as their Lord and Savior."

Many children believe in fairytales or the lies they are told by their parents about these celebrated fictional characters of this world. However, our children must come to know God, their *Dad, and Difference Maker* for themselves in this ever-increasing wicked and perverse world! My words of concern and truth that I wanted my sons to hear from me was that they must be godly fathers, Dads as Difference Makers pointing their children to the God I introduced them to. Even so, to my *Daddy* and God, who I now know so much better than I did when my sons were under my care.

The Physical and Spiritual Imprint of a Father

For a godly dad, it should be his deepest desire and earnest longing that his offspring, who had no choice in receiving his DNA or biological imprint, would one day choose of their own volition to embrace the love and lordship of their daddy's *Daddy* – God the Heavenly Father (Deuteronomy 6:6,7). As a Dad lovingly guides his children in spiritual truth, teaching them to revere God, he plants seeds of faith and trust while he endlessly prays that the Word of God he shares with them may one day take root in their hearts. Thus, leading the child gifted to him into an intimate or personal relationship with their Creator and *Daddy* (Proverbs 22:6).

It should go without saying, however, because of the fallen world we are born into and are one with terrestrially, I must say, that a father's role does not end at conception. While a man's physical life-seed, shared with his wife, creates a new life, his responsibilities as a father must go far beyond this moment. This new life, shaped by the biological union of father and mother, carries an imprint of both parents – a genetic and physical foundation that forms the child's early development and identity. Yet, many fathers fall short of fulfilling their full role (Ephesians 6:4). They may contribute to the physical creation of life but fail to impart the wisdom, guidance, and spiritual truths that shape the hearts and souls of their children and, of most importance, their potential as true imagers of God.

This dual imprint – a physical legacy combined with a father's influence – has lasting effects. The child reflects their parents' physical beauty and biological traits but also bears the inherent flaws of human nature – a sinful disposition passed down through generations. The presence of sin within the world and the challenges or dilemmas brought head-on before a godly dad should remind him to embrace his calling as a godly leader or else fail in his responsibility, leaving his child[ren] vulnerable to the destructive forces of this world (1Peter 5:8).

For a man of faith, this journey of fatherhood begins with his own spiritual renewal. Just as his physical union with his wife brings forth a new life, his spiritual union with the Holy Spirit creates new life within him (1 Corinthians 5:17). Born again as a child of God, he is recreated and renewed in the likeness of his Heavenly Father. He now bears not only a physical responsibility but also a spiritual duty – a command to reflect God's character in his home. This transformed father, empowered by the Holy Spirit, is then equipped to lead his family with love, integrity, and humility (Micah 6:8). Now, as Dad the Difference Maker, he partners with the Holy Spirit to guide his children toward his *Dad*, teaching them to know their Heavenly Father through his own example (Matthew 6:19-21).

In a godly marriage, a father's calling becomes even more significant. It is not enough for him to provide physically; he must also leave a lasting, godly impression that transcends the temporary things of this world. His deepest desire should be that his children, who had no choice in receiving his DNA, would one day choose freely to embrace the love and lordship of their Heavenly Father. As Dad the Difference Maker models a life of faith, he nurtures in his children an understanding of God's love and truth, planting seeds of faith that they may one day embrace eternal life offered through Jesus.

And so, a godly father's prayer is that his children would see God not only as their Creator but as their true Father, their *Daddy and Difference Maker*, who loves them infinitely and personally. This is not a journey he can force; it is a path he must prepare, laying a foundation of faith and trust that his children might freely choose (Joshua 24:15). He knows that only God can ultimately call his children to Himself, yet a godly father willingly takes on the role of a shepherd or guide, pointing them to the Heavenly

Father through Jesus, the Son, who is the exact image or *Spiritual DNA* of God, His Father.

A father who has come to see the beauty and blessing of holiness – the very essence of God's nature – seeks to embody this holiness for his children. He becomes a living example of love, humility, and godliness, and it is through this example that he fulfills his calling. His children see in him a reflection of their Heavenly Father, a glimpse of *Abba* or *Daddy*, and begin to understand what it means to live a life transformed by God's Spirit.

Recognizing that his own time on earth is only for a moment, this heavenly-bound father dedicates himself to raising his children to walk in faith. He knows that one day, he will be united with his *Daddy* in heaven. Therefore, his greatest and prayerful hope is that his children will join him, they too having chosen to become one with God and reflecting His image. A Daddy's heart should long for his children to become heirs of an eternal kingdom, disciples of Christ, and image-bearers of their Heavenly Father.

As demonstrated, a godly dad is much more than a biological parent; he is a spiritual leader and an earthly shepherd, guiding his family toward a heavenly home. His true and unfading legacy is not measured by earthly success or wealth but by the eternal truths he has received from the Holy Spirit and, in return, has sown in his offspring's hearts. Having become a godly dad and king of his home, he understands that his greatest responsibility is to lead his children to a new life rooted in Christ. In every word and action, he strives to be Dad the Difference Maker – the godly influence that will guide his children toward their true Father, their *Ultimate Dad, the Difference Maker.*

Yet, when a father neglects this role – choosing to live by the world's standards or for his own desires – he aligns himself with Dad the Dilemma – the Devil himself. As previously mentioned, he may provide physically, but he fails to offer the spiritual leadership his family so desperately needs. In this abdication, he becomes an instrument of confusion – Dad the Dilemma, thereby leaving his children spiritually vulnerable and detached from the knowledge of their Heavenly Father.

A father, therefore, stands at a crossroads. His life and legacy will either reflect the nature of Dad the Difference Maker or become an embodiment of Dad the Dilemma (Deuteronomy 30:19). His choice – to walk in step with the Heavenly Father or to turn away – determines the spiritual path he sets for his family. And it is this choice that shapes not only his children's earthly lives but also their eternal understanding of their Heavenly Father.

CHAPTER 5

Daddy's Need for Their Dads

When a man grows up without a father, most assuredly some developmental lack and void forms that often follow him throughout his life. I'm not speaking from some distant, theoretical understanding – I'm speaking as a man who has lived it. Fathers, we need to understand something foundational: when dads are **MAA** (Missing After Action), we can become detrimental dilemmas to ourselves and others. Many carry around scars and silent struggles, unspoken pain that echoes through our lives. We walk through the world burdened by questions that should have been answered by the steady presence of a father, by his love, guidance, and discipline. Without him, we stumble into adulthood as broken men.

A dad without a dad of his own often wrestles with thoughts like, "You did this to me." This blame can shape our very identity, hardening us against the world, the people in our lives, and even our own children. As Daddy Dilemmas, men may unknowingly pass down this brokenness to our families, leaving them to pick up the pieces of an emotional heritage we inherited ourselves.

The truth is, a broken dad can't help but project his own pain onto his family, leaving a trail of wounds that don't just affect him but extend to every relationship he holds dear. Children growing up in such an environment and becoming maladjusted adults may come to a bitter realization, saying, "Dad, you further damaged me," this being apart from one's innate sin struggles. This isn't just a story about broken fathers – it's about broken families, broken hearts, and a broken legacy that can span generations.

There's A Hole in My Soul

Giving thought to Fred Hammond's words: "There's a hole in my soul that won't heal. There's a rage and a pain, even now, I still feel. Even though I'm a man, I still don't understand, but that's what happens when you don't have a father." When I reflect on these words, I give thought to the countless sons and daughters who feel exactly this – a hole so deep that no amount of success, achievement, or busyness can fill it. The pain is real, the rage festers, and the absence remains. That is the cost of fatherlessness!

No person was designed to walk through life bearing the weight of such a loss. This isn't just something we can "get over." It leaves lasting wounds, ones that show up in our lives in ways we may not even recognize until it's too late. I'm inclined to believe that many of our youth are destructive and violent, not merely because they aren't being disciplined. But rather, as the lyricist stated, "the rage and pain" and other negative feelings that a fatherless child often, if not daily, grapple with, and in many cases act out and even lose to this spiritual warfare! Don't think that this burden goes unnoticed by God.

For every man who thinks he can live life absent from his children or only partially present, I remind you that there is a God who will hold us accountable. We can't outrun the responsibility of being a father. We will be judged for the legacy we leave, whether it's one of love or neglect, of faithfulness or failure. God's design for fatherhood is clear and intentional; it is not a role we can take lightly or abandon without consequences. When we, as fathers, neglect our duties or harm our children through our absence or brokenness, we will answer to the Almighty.

Struggling Fathers and Husbands: You Can't Give What You Did Not Receive

Then there are men who long to be husbands and fathers but never had the example they needed. They step into marriage wanting to be a "good man" to create the family they never had, but something fundamental is missing. A father who was never fathered is often unequipped to fulfill the role of husband or dad. I've met men who carry this longing for connection but lack the skills to sustain it. Without a relationship with their Heavenly Father – or a respectable and loving earthly dad, they struggle, unable to give what they never received. These men want marriage and family, but without that guiding presence, they are left fumbling in the dark. The hard truth is that wanting to be a good husband or father is not enough. It requires a foundation, one that begins with a relationship with God and, ideally, with the example of a godly father – a Dad and Difference Maker.

And, so, there is this ache, this unfulfilled longing for a dad that, for some, never goes away or fades. I know that ache because it showed up painfully a couple of times when I was a young man and also a dad and husband. Looking back, I can see that I spent my 20s and 30s searching for someone to fill that void. There were these two unforgettable times when the need for my dad's presence was so strong it felt like a physical pain. Cal Scott was the father that I loved and the only "dad" that I knew until my mother told me otherwise just before I entered High School. I will address or dress this matter of my unique Daddy Dilemmas to include an unexpected paternal revelation soon enough.

As for these two unforgettable experiences that I also mentioned in my first book, first, the latter of the two: I was sitting at an intersection, gripped by a wave of longing for my dad that I couldn't shake. It seemed to have come out of nowhere, like a heavy weight pressing down on me, reminding me of my suppressed yearning for my dad. My inner man cried out from within, or maybe I actually verbalized my longing; I don't remember which, but my outcry was, "I want my daddy!" I was in my early to mid-thirties when this occurred.

Regarding my earliest recall and occurrence or such intense longing, it was during the summer of *nineteen eighty-six*. I'd recently completed my military service and had turned *21 years of age*. And now I was standing in the cemetery of Glenview Memorial Park. I had gone there to find my dad, Cal's marker, to, in some manner, attempt to find a measure of consolation from a dad who I clearly knew was gone, with whom I also knew I had absolutely no access. During this season of my life and the first of such an experience, I felt tremendously lost and unsure about my future. I was there alone, surrounded by silence and stones marking lives that had come and gone. I call it my *Graveyard Experience* because, in that moment, I felt as if part of me had died, too.

Sobbing deeply, I stood there, fatherless and vulnerable, feeling every ounce of that loneliness and loss as I longed for my dad. It was a visceral ache that went beyond words, a realization that I was alone in this world. Those were the moments that showed me just how deep the need for a father really is. Fatherless, I stood there – a grown man with an empty space in my heart that should have been filled by the **one** who brought me into this world.

To the mothers reading this, please know this is no disrespect to you. You are cherished, your sacrifices are acknowledged, and your strength is deeply respected. Many of you have raised children without the help of your child's father, and you have done so with grace, love, and resilience. I honor you for that. But please hear me when I say this: no matter how strong you are or have or had been, you cannot replace the role of a man and what has been purposed by God for the child's dad to help complete or to bring balance to his child and the life they are to live.

Mothers, you may be doing everything within your power, giving all of yourself to your children, but there is a place in a child's heart or innate reasoning that only a father can fill. This truth may be hard to accept, but it needs to be said in a changing world with its "alternative" lifestyle choices where fathers are often dismissed as secondary. The love of a mother is profound, but it is not the same as the love of a father. God designed it that way so that you two, together with God's guidance, may, in fact, bring completeness and balance to this gift of a child that God has entrusted to each of you equally to love and care for according to your distinct roles and design.

For me, since the age of *twelve,* when Cal divorced himself from his family, this journey of fatherlessness has been a long one, with moments of emptiness and often deep loneliness. Now, nearing the age of *sixty,* I look back on those years of longing, of searching, of standing at that intersection and that graveyard, and I see how these experiences shaped me. But through it all, I have come to understand something crucial: though my earthly dad[s] was absent, my Heavenly Father has always been with me. He has been my guide, my protector, my source of strength. And as I share this with you, I hope it brings a measure of comfort to those of you walking a similar path. Your pain is real, and your longing is valid. But you are not alone, *Dad, our Difference Maker,* and God is standing before you to show you his love for you!

I now want every man, dad, and husband to consider what kind of legacy you are leaving behind. Are you a man who will be remembered as a "dilemma," someone who added to the brokenness of those around you? Or will you be a man who is present, loving, and devoted, leaving a legacy of healing and strength to those under your influence and/or care? A broken man says, "You did this to me," casting blame on the world and everyone else. But a man restored by God says, "*Daddy,* you did this for me" (John 3:16; Romans 5:8; Galatians 4:6; 1 John 3:1). He sees those under his influence or a dad his children as gifts, as blessings that shape him and make him a better man – hence a Difference Maker! To the fathers who want to break the cycle of brokenness, who want to be "Difference Makers" rather than dilemmas, know that it starts with surrender. Surrender to God. Seek Him as your true Father, and allow Him to heal the wounds you carry.

Essentially, what has been expressed thus far is for all of us who are fatherless, for those of us who are fathers now, and for those sons and daughters still carrying the weight of a father's absence; fathers, your children need you to be present in their lives. They need your heart, your guidance, your love. If we are to raise up a generation that knows God, understands love, and feels secure in their identity, it starts with us – godly men, imagers of our heavenly Father, who, like Jesus and our example as a kingdom Son and King Himself, must be about our Father's business (Luke 2:49; John 6:38 & 17:4).

Fathers, let's be the Difference Makers that our Creator has purposed us to become. Let's leave behind more than our names or our DNA to fatherless children and *Mama Drama* because you chose to become **MAA.** Let's leave a legacy of faith, strength, and love rooted in the *One* who *Fathered* us all. In accepting God as our *Daddy the Difference Maker,* in this He is well pleased! On the other hand, to reject Him, one remains as one with their daddy, the Devil; therefore, sin or all sorts of evil will reign over you as you, knowingly or not, as Satan's sons and even his fathers sinfully victimize others (Romans 6:16; 2 Corinthians 4:4).

Sins of the Fathers

Up to this point, I don't think I could have made the matter of sin's awful effect upon each of us, as well as because of us, much clearer. Nevertheless, here's a reminder before I address the subject, *Sins of the Fathers.* Before we came to know Jesus as our Lord and Savior, according to the Bible, each of us was viewed as enemies of God because of our sinful condition and disposition (Romans 5:10); we all were, therefore, earmarked for eternal damnation in the *Lake of Fire* (Revelation 20:15)!

What wrongs we did or did not do, how minimum our sinful misconduct was, or how egregious and deplorable, we all were in the same boat as inherently sin-sick people in need of healing and deliverance (Romans 3:23; Isaiah 64:6)! Thanks be to God our *Daddy, the Ultimate Difference Maker,* that no matter our past sins of indiscretion or malicious calculation to commit evil, in Jesus, we all are now seen as Difference Makers, sons and daughters of our Father who has redeemed us and forgiven us for our trespasses (Ephesians 1:7; 2 Corinthians 5:17). Even so, we, as children of God, have been commanded to forgive others (Colossians 3:13). Amen!

In this book and more so in my previous book, I chose to discuss, in particular, the ugliness and folly of my sinful behavior. However, collectively, the wrongs, shortcomings, or failures of those who are forever linked to me, biologically or otherwise. As indicated, we all are sin-sick and are in need of deliverance and the enablement of the Holy Spirit to live righteously before our *Dad* and Creator.

As I've shared my truth and story, my intention has not been to condemn anyone but rather to show the harm that we can bring to others while we remain in our brokenness; even so, the danger we are to ourselves and those created in God's image... Yes, we all belong to and are held accountable before God no matter what state of disrepair or deliverance and sanctification we are in. Just the same, it is God's love for us, His mercy and patience towards us, that He wants all who will to be restored to Him as Difference Makers.

Giving thought to my past, I see a pattern – a legacy shaped by the men in my life who, in some manner, directly and indirectly, despite their intentions, also passed on brokenness as much as they passed on their influence, their names, if not their name, their DNA. Each of these men is now deceased. The first of these men that I was acquainted with was Cal Scott – my dad, the man I was led to believe was my biological father until I was about fifteen years of age. Cal was a good man in many ways, but he was also a rolling stone; clarity of this distinction can be understood from the song bearing the title, "Papa Was a Rollin' Stone,' which was introduced to the world by the musical group, The Temptations.

My dad's life, like so many others, was marked by a tragic absence: he never knew his father, who was also a Daddy Dilemma who additionally had struggles of his own. But Cal may have seen him in passing or engaged him in brief conversation when he was a young child. If my recall is correct, Cal may have barely been a teenager, if that, when his dad died. Without that foundation of a father, I can only begin to imagine the challenges that my dad faced and that followed him into numerical manhood.

Cal married my mother under less than favorable conditions for her; initially, his motivation was selfish to say the least. My mother later told me she was informed years after the fact that this was so. Through this union, I became his adopted son around the age of two. Mention and more detail about my siblings are in my first book. Therefore, I will not provide any additional elaboration here. Although my dad grew to care for my mother, moreover a genuinely good man, he struggled deeply with his own weaknesses, which I also witnessed firsthand, as shared in my previous book as well.

Regarding my mother, there was clearly *Mama Drama* because Cal was the product of his Daddy Dilemma. From what I gather, my dad also lacked a personal relationship with God, which left him vulnerable, wrestling with desires he couldn't control and passions that led him down paths of infidelity. Even so, my dad led me by his words and through his actions down paths that created dilemmas for me as well. To date, we are aware that Cal has children from three different women; sadly, there could be more.

Additionally, there was another man who I recalled as being a friendly person when I was a child but who negatively affected me in my later years, Linwood Bullock. It was he whom my mother informed me was my "biological father" as I was about to begin High School. And from whom my given middle name, Lynn, is a derivative of his first name. Like Cal, he, too, was a rolling stone, with children by no less than four different women.

While my mother was pregnant with me, at the time the two were "dating," Linwood also had his wife pregnant, a fact unknown to my mother at the time...that he was also married. Linwood's actions only added layers of confusion and pain to an already complex story and *Mama Drama!* In time, he went on to father at least one other child while in his second marriage, creating an echo of unresolved issues, struggles, or cascading dilemmas throughout each child's life and all who cared for his offspring.

The weight of his actions created a ripple effect, impacting everyone involved, not the least of which my mother, who had to bear the burden of his lies and secret life. Linwood, much like Cal, was a man who, as best as I know, neither anchored himself in faith toward Jesus my Savior. And as a result, he, too, was a dilemma – a man whose choices left a legacy of pain rather than peace. Unlike Cal, from what I understand, Linwood did have his dad, who was present throughout his life. I will, therefore, reason that Linwood became a Daddy Dilemma because he was a slave to his passion – hence, sin had mastery over him.

Then, there was Jim Waring, the man who provided his DNA for my youngest sibling. Before I went off to the Army, my home was also the place where he laid his head. Jim, too, had his character flaws, flaws that impacted my mother – more *Mama Drama* and subsequently his actions that deeply affected me at the time but also until this day. I don't recall much about his personal life or upbringing; admittedly, I don't really care to know. Here's why. While I was in the military stationed at Fort Bragg, now known as Fort Liberty, I remember talking to my mother via a phone call.

My mother was crying as she informed me of his blatant disrespect and his harsh and demeaning words towards her that hurt me to the core. Traveling home from Fort Bragg, it was my intention to hurt him back, to retaliate, to make him feel pain because he caused my mother pain! Standing outside of his apartment with a stick that I had handpicked that was as large as a baseball bat, but longer, I had intended to inflict harm upon him and damage his property.

But even as a young man filled with such rage, I could not bring myself to go that far. It just wasn't in my soul to harm him, no matter how much I despised his actions and hated him! Looking back, I see how God held me back from crossing that line, even when my pain and anger seemed overwhelming. As I shared in my previous book, I came to embrace Jesus while I was going through military boot camp.

This incident with Jim took place about a year after my baptism into the death and resurrection of Jesus, my *Difference Maker*. Ironically, the church where I was baptized, Greater Saint Paul, Durham, N.C., by the late Pastor, W.T. Bigelow, could be readily viewed from Jim's apartment, which was less than half a block in distance from where I stood that night, threatening and cursing Jim, who refused to step outside. That night, I was faced with a potentially disastrous Daddy Dilemma, but God stood before me and between us as my *Daddy, the Difference Maker!* O, for the grace and mercy of God! By the way, Jim has at least two children by different women.

The sins of these fathers and/or father figures either influenced or shaped me; call it as you will. But they certainly left an indelible mark on me: I remember as a teenager also boldly calling out Cal and standing against him because of the emotional pain he caused my mother. When this occurred, I was sitting on my sister's bed. His response... He reared back his right fist. With his left hand, he grabbed me behind my head to inflict maximum suffering on me as he was poised to strike me in the face. Then he came to his senses.

If Cal had hit me... let me also mention that my sister was sitting beside me, his other adopted child. Because of his sheer strength, he would have killed me; if not killed me, he would have permanently disfigured my face and caused me lasting emotional trauma, if not brain damage as well. My sister would have certainly been more traumatized if his anger had not abated. This was the last time I saw my dad. I had now enlisted in the army. While stationed at Bragg, I received a call informing me that my dad had died in a trucking accident. I'd never stopped loving him, but clearly, he was a conflicted and broken man! I also remember thinking and wondering, after receiving the report of my Dad's death, if he was *Saved*. I then prayed as best as I understood how, at the time, that he was Saved or would be Saved.

During this time, I knew Linwood was my biological father. I, therefore, expected him to show up and man up after my dad had died. Beforehand, and sporadically, Linwood would extend what I called cameo appearances to me; at the time, I didn't mind. This continued to be how he operated once I'd gotten out of the army. However, he then elected to rather act as a coward. His disregard for his grandson and me, furthermore the concern or fear that he had in his eyes when I saw him in public with his other family, said it all... His facial expression pleaded to me, "Please don't approach my family and acknowledge me." I experienced this reaction from him a couple of times. However, later in life, I chose to visit his home; my wife was with me. He came to the door, followed by his wife. He stood cowardly silent like a deer frozen by the headlights of a car. What a dilemma he was faced with!

His wife then started going off on me! As I slowly stepped off the porch while attempting to calmly break his trance of silence while also respectfully engaging his wife... he said nothing. His wife continues to forcefully demand that I leave. As I am slowly retreating to accommodate her demands, I am also looking at Linwood. He then speaks. His words to me were, "I think it's best that you leave." I am quite certain this was the last time I saw him. Sometime later, he succumbed to cancer.

Because of Linwood's actions or inaction, as laid out before you, I totally lost respect for him. It wasn't until much later, I am pretty sure after Linwood's death, that my sister, his biological daughter, shared with me that she, too, on one occasion, was disregarded by him when he was with his family. This came as quite a surprise to my sister because they communicated with regularity. As for me, we were cordial when we encountered one another in passing or the one or two times when he came by my home.

However, after I observed his cowardliness, I, emotionally and otherwise, cut him off even though I still thought that he was my biological father. I could say more; however, the only thing that I will add is that since Linwood's passing, his family and I have been cordial when we encounter each other in passing. Linwood as a Daddy Dilemma certainly had a rippling effect on many, in particular his offspring, his seed and DNA making. And in his death, he still does... what a dilemma!

Lastly, I will make mention of Jim. I don't think I'd actually laid eyes on him since I lived with my mother, which was before I went to the Army. I certainly had not spoken to him. Years had passed, perhaps two decades. He is now sickly and hospital-bound. My mother didn't seem to hold his failures as a man or dad against him; besides, they had a child in common. Jim was gravely ill, and my mother informed me that Jim wanted to see me. By this time, I was licensed as a preacher and had been for around two decades.

Admittedly, I had no desire, none at all, to see him. I didn't carry hate towards him. However, now, as he lies on his deathbed, he wants to see me. I didn't see the point in it. If he got his life right with Jesus, well and fine. I think it's worth pointing out that my mother actually met him at Greater Saint Paul; how ironic. When they started seeing one another, I remember her mentioning to me that he sang in the choir. Each of these men was already Dilemmas when my mother met them. However, she was incapable of discerning this at the time. But neither had my mother known her dad that she may receive his guidance and love. The man who had become her step-father, as I've been told, he was also a hell of a Dilemma!

It is worth noting that I recognize the ghastly mistreatment of our ancestors by Europeans who settled in this country. Their satanic system of enslavement of people of African heritage has, in large part, through its rippling effect, greatly contributed to the struggles of African American men. An egregious system that further aimed to divide and destroy African American families! We must not forget – this horrible system of European slavery's aftermath continues to be felt today! However, as godly men and Dads who are Difference Makers, one family at a time, we can make a difference!

There is yet one final fraternal linkage that I've been vaguely alluding to. A unique and, for some, what was and perhaps remains for others, a disturbing Daddy Dilemma to my story that came to light as a result of my taking a DNA test. I'd finished writing my first book and was in the final editing phase when this revelation presented itself. It was my intention to write this companion book that you are now reading.

However, at the time, what I now know, I did not know. What I did not know and in these unknowns because my story or findings had not brought me closure. But rather unanswered and perhaps questions never to be answered… such was my thinking. I was met with no path or knowledge about my history or my complete identity. I was now faced with an identity crisis that many daily struggle with! For this reason, I now know that many turn to DNA testing to try to find answers.

My reason for taking the DNA test, I simply wanted to explore my heritage to understand what part of Africa I originated from. What I discovered – hence now know, however, was far more consequential than I or anyone expected. As I've shared, my mother informed me that Cal Scott was not my biological father. Moreover, resulting from DNA testing, I also discovered neither was Linwood Bullock. Through my DNA test, I learned that I was, in fact, paternally a Barnett. This revelation was both surprising and oddly fitting, as the last piece of a puzzle to my life that I hadn't realized was incomplete. In my discovery, I felt a strange mixture of loss and clarity – a loss for the identity I'd carried for so long and clarity about the legacy that was truly mine. And even uncertainty about my hope to leave a legacy.

Loveless Conception

My discovery of my biological identity as a Barnett brought with it another surprise. A young woman, Halimah, my "niece," so she initially concluded, reached out to me because of our DNA match via Ancestry DNA testing. She'd seen my name and match with hers through our test results and was as quite surprised as I was. Her life now included me. Whereas my life's history would be rewritten by the discovery. Here was this niece I had never known, now forever connected to me by blood, by heritage, and by the circumstances beyond our control that had biologically brought us into the world.

As we talked, with a limited understanding of this testing process, I attempted to piece together and make sense of a story I never knew was mine. I realized that my conception was not what I'd thought or could have imagined. It was, in a shockingly profound manner, a loveless conception – rape, a product of circumstances that left its mark on both our lives and painfully upon my mother; more on this is forthcoming. As for my newly discovered niece, she believed that this revelation brought her an uncle. Yet, for me, it brought something deeper – a grounding in the truth of who I might possibly be according to paternal lineage. I was born paternally not as a Scott, nor as a Bullock, but as a Barnett. Yet even in that realization, as a child of God, I came to understand that my identity transcends bloodlines and surnames.

The truth is, while my biology may link me to the Barnetts, my true identity is found in something and *Someone* infinitely greater. I am not solely defined by my earthly lineage or my physical heritage. *My identity – my real and eternal distinctive personage, is in Jesus alone!* I am not merely a product of my earthly progenitor's choices and DNA. *But instead, a child of God, born again and made new spiritually.* Biologically, I may be a Barnett; nevertheless, spiritually, I am renewed. *I am a son of God, claimed and redeemed by Him (2 Corinthians 6:18)!*

The circumstances of my earthly birth may be complicated for some to grasp, but my rebirth in Christ had beforehand given me clarity, purpose, and peace. *And so, I knew my true identity before I received my DNA report – I knew that I was the child of a King... Jesus is His name! Therefore, regardless of how I got here, through Jesus, my (our) new name and identity reign supreme over everything! Life's circumstances... they can never define nor hinder me! Why?... because I belong to the King!*

This life's journey, though filled with unexpected twists and revelations, has led me to one simple truth: my true identity is in God, my *Daddy, the Ultimate Difference Maker (John 1:12)!* I am His, born again from above and in this truth, I find rest and eternal comfort. No matter where I came from, no matter the sins of the fathers or the failings of the men who shaped my life, I know who I am. I am defined not by my past, my father's or mother's DNA mixture, but by my Savior, Jesus (2 Corinthians 5:17)! If your life's story and circumstances mirror mine. I pray that in and through Jesus, you embrace and establish your new identity. He longs to call you His own!

CHAPTER 6

Let's Talk DNA - Let the DNA Talk

On June 28, 2019, I took a small step that would connect me to generations past – a simple submission of my DNA to Ancestry. The journey I was about to embark upon was for me to connect with my African origins. The question of where I come from, who my ancestors were, and what stories their lives could tell lingered in my mind. Because African Americans were stolen and sold from their homeland, unlike other Americans who make up this melting pot, many of us know little to nothing about their African heritage… And so, I wanted to discover mine.

Just a few weeks later, on July 11, 2019, I received confirmation that Ancestry had received my sample. And then, on Aug 1, 2019, it happened – my DNA results were ready, a digital link between me and generations of people who came before me. As I opened those results, I felt a rush of excitement and curiosity. To my delight, the breakdown of my ancestry spoke of a vivid mosaic of African heritage and a tapestry woven with both the familiar and the unexpected. At the core of my DNA was Nigeria, making up a significant 28% of my heritage. This was my predominant African lineage, linking me to the vibrant and resilient people of Nigeria. I felt an instant kinship.

The journey didn't stop there. I discovered that 13% of my lineage came from Benin and Togo, another deep-rooted tie to the African continent. This connection hinted at ancestral ties along the western coast, to lands rich in culture, music, and traditions that have endured despite the tests of time. My DNA also pointed me to Senegal and Cameroon, each contributing 8%. These regions further expanded my understanding of the rich diversity of my heritage.

My ancestral roots stretched into Ghana and the Ivory Coast as well, with each contributing 6% of my DNA. This part of West Africa, known for its powerful kingdoms and enduring traditions, was part of my lineage. Central West Africa, also making up 6%, brought another layer of African identity, hinting at the resilience and strength of people who lived in what we now know as Angola and other surrounding regions. And then came traces of Europe, 6% of my DNA came from Germanic Europe, and 5% from England and Northwestern Europe. I could only begin to imagine how I might have acquired European DNA... My limited thoughts, African enslavement, and the sexual abuse of my female ancestors. However, I did wonder if there were, perhaps, loving and consensual relationships that caused my DNA to be so colorful or mixed.

But my DNA journey didn't end there. The Western Bantu people of Southern Africa were a part of me as well, making up 4% of my ancestry, with 3% from Mali and 3% from North Central Nigeria. The details became even more intricate with a 3% connection to the Nigerian woodlands. Wales contributed 2%, and even the Indigenous Americas North left a trace, with 1% of my DNA hinting at a shared history across continents and peoples.

Every percentage in this DNA breakdown was more than just a number; it was a story, a chapter in a long, complex history of movement, resilience, adaptation, and survival. Each piece of my heritage, each region represented, was part of a larger story. My DNA doesn't just speak of the past; it is a bridge to understanding who I am biologically. In exploring my DNA, I found a profound sense of identity, a unique blend of African origins and global connections. This journey allowed me to see myself as part of a living history, one that continues through me and into future generations. The knowledge of these origins has only deepened my appreciation for the lives that shaped mine, and it has inspired me to honor their stories in my own journey forward.

After receiving my DNA Ancestry report, I was filled with the joy of learning about my origins. The intricate web of African, European, and Indigenous people, aka "American Indian" roots, provided a sense of belonging, a connection to people and places I could now identify as my own. But beyond the excitement of discovering my heritage, I hadn't anticipated that my DNA results would offer more than just a history lesson. Little did I realize they could also connect me with people I'd never met – family members whose lives had been a mystery to me until now.

In the year that followed, I received a couple of messages from people who had found me through Ancestry. They wondered about our shared heritage or familial connection, though I didn't know who they were or how we might be related. I was somewhat surprised and honestly, unfamiliar with how Ancestry worked in this way. The idea of finding living relatives (a few I have since established a relationship with) across the miles, of possibly piecing together long-lost family branches, was something I had not considered or yet fully grasped with regard to DNA testing.

Then, almost a year and a half after I received my results, something unexpected happened. On December 1, 2020, I received a message via Ancestry from an individual – Halimah, who introduced herself as my "niece," although the Ancestry report also indicated that she may be a first cousin. She reached out via Ancestry Messenger so that we may discuss her findings. In her initial message, she shared that we were related and explained that her mother was seeking to connect with her maternal family. Halimah added a word of caution. She stated to me if we move forward to explore more that, this could open up a "Pandora's Box." This wasn't just another inquiry; Halimah was certain that we were closely connected.

Without reservation, I responded, "I'm all about what is true." I warmly welcomed the opportunity to connect with someone who might indeed be family. I responded to Halimah, expressing my openness to exploring this relationship further. The concept of DNA linking us in this way was still somewhat foreign to me, and while I trusted science, I felt the need to understand more fully how this process worked.

When I expressed this to Halimah, she replied simply: "The DNA is what it is. The DNA doesn't lie." I responded, "I'm not questioning the results; I simply need to understand the process. For years, I had identified one man as my biological father, had seen my lineage through that lens, and had framed my life story around that knowledge. Now, here was DNA suggesting otherwise, hinting at a story beneath the surface, a narrative yet to be unraveled.

In the days and few weeks that followed, I continued my conversations with Halimah and her mother. I even expressed interest in immediately traveling to Georgia to meet Halimah's mother – my "sister," so Halimah concluded at the time. Halimah shared an observation that would later give me pause regarding her mother being my sister. She mentioned that on her DNA match page, another family member was listed just before my name. This individual, she said, was her uncle, and it was confirmed based on their DNA connection. Given his proximity to my name on her match list, she speculated that if he was her uncle, then I must also be her uncle. Halimah suggested that her mother was my sister and that her grandfather would, therefore, be my father. At this time, her grandfather had been deceased for several years.

Her words left me intrigued! I had set out on this journey to learn about my ancestry, but now I was standing at the brink of a discovery that could reshape my entire understanding of my immediate family. If Halimah was correct, if her mother was indeed my sister, then her grandfather – the man she called her grandfather – could very well be my father. I welcomed this revelation.

The thought of uncovering a sister and a father I had never known was at once thrilling and surreal. Initially, Halimah and her mother were more than willing to help fill in the gaps. A short time later, Halimah's mother – shared photos of their patriarch. I examined the images carefully, studying the face of the man who might indeed be my biological father.

As I looked at his face, I couldn't deny the resemblance. Even his ears and beard were like mine. There were features we shared, traits that seemed more than mere coincidence. I saw traces of myself in him. I had no reason to believe that this wasn't my progenitor. This journey was no longer just about discovering my African roots – it was leading me toward answers I hadn't even thought to question.

With the information and limited understanding that I had acquired regarding DNA testing, I was finally prepared to bring forth this information to my mother and siblings. I knew that this would be a challenging time for my mother! However, I thought that once I presented and carefully articulated what I'd discovered, she would be welcoming and eager to travel with me along this journey of discovery. I was sorely mistaken! I also underestimated that two of my siblings would not readily embrace taking a DNA test to help sort out a critical aspect of our thought-to-be-shared lineage or story.

I could add so much more about this experience with family members that I didn't expect to encounter due to this dilemma before us all. Although relevant to the themes of this book, however, not of necessity to be told. Therefore, I will omit these details but briefly touch on the matter shortly. Perhaps the following will give you some insight into my journey of discovery and truth involving family: I had two family members who suggested, not to me directly, that "I had lost my mind… and that I was, in fact, crazy," one of which was my mother. My persistence to find my truth was relentless and unwavering! In the end, the truth exonerated me!

Nevertheless, this Daddy Dilemma caused pain that may not have totally dissipated for all involved. And perhaps never will. Through all of this, and in the midst of it all, I was good. As a family, we are now good!

Unraveling the Threads: A DNA's Journey Unexpected Turns

As I delved deeper into understanding the DNA testing process, a clearer picture began to emerge. With each new insight, it became apparent that my biological connection to Halimah was not as straightforward as she had initially thought and that I had wholeheartedly embraced. Early on, Halimah had believed that her mother was my sister and that her grandfather was my father. But as I learned more about the science behind DNA matches, I realized that things didn't line up as neatly as we'd hoped.

A crucial detail shifted the landscape of our understanding: I was not a DNA match with Halimah's uncle, whose name was just above mine on her Ancestry family listing. This absence of connection raised questions for me, suggesting that the family lines we'd presumed were connecting us were now in question. Yet, the mystery wasn't entirely resolved as we were left to speculate about this miscalculation. There remained an undeniable link between Halimah and me, one that persisted despite the apparent discrepancies in our lineage.

One piece of evidence that kept me searching was the presence of a shared match. The name Lisa Barnett appeared on both our DNA match lists, a name that bridged our separate family histories. It was a new clue, something tangible we could both hold onto as we tried to make sense of our connection. The appearance of Lisa Barnett in both our family lines hinted at a story beyond the one Halimah had believed to be true.

As these revelations unfolded, it became apparent that the story Halimah had held close might not align with what was biologically verifiable. The man she had called her father – the history she'd known and cherished – might not be the full picture of her origins. This moment was pivotal for both of us. For me, it was a revelation that turned my search for heritage into a shared journey toward truth. For Halimah, it raised questions that were likely both enlightening and challenging, reshaping the landscape of her family story.

Amid these DNA discoveries, Halimah also found herself navigating her own life challenges. She informed me with the responsibilities of motherhood and marriage pressing upon her, she chose to pause our discussions. I was quite bothered by her abrupt decision; I responded to her, "You brought me into this situation, and now you're taking a break, and you will get back to me later!" I wanted her to clearly know that her decision to press pause did not sit well with me. This journey was proving more complex and layered than either of us had anticipated! It seemed to me that she needed time to process what these DNA findings could mean for her own sense of identity.

So, as Halimah took a step back, I, too, found myself at a crossroads. Our efforts together were not temporally suspended but altogether ceased, but my journey to discovery wasn't over. The answers might take time, but the journey toward understanding the depths of our shared DNA would continue. The pursuit to understand my heritage through DNA continued to unfold in unexpected ways. As I sought to unravel the threads of my family history, shortly after hearing from Halimah, I reached out to Lisa Barnett 28 days later, on December 2020. Given that Lisa was a shared match for both Halimah and me, I hoped that a conversation with her might shed some light on how our lives were intertwined. I reached out to her through Ancestry Messenger, eager to establish a connection that might lead to answers.

Lisa responded, but the conversation did not go as I had hoped. She was searching for information herself, but her interests did not align with the questions I was asking her. She wasn't sure about the nature of our connection. Besides, her search was unlike mine; she was seeking answers maternally; therefore, at the time, she was not concerned with how we intersected. Our conversation was brief, and it quickly became apparent that Lisa was either unable or unwilling to continue discussing our DNA connection. This was another disappointment and setback for me!

Undeterred, I pressed on, determined to piece together whatever information I could find. In May of 2021, I decided to try a different approach. I reached out to a couple of people on Lisa's Facebook account. Both were willing to assist; however, Pam Clay Mealer was more instrumental. To my relief, Pam was open to speaking with me. I explained my situation, sharing the unexpected journey my DNA test had set me on and the questions I had about Lisa Barnett.

Pam listened and was receptive, expressing genuine interest in helping me understand the connections that had surfaced. She mentioned that she knew the Barnett family. Pam shared with me that her parents and Fred Barnett's parents had been good friends and worked together for many years. Her familiarity with the family offered a glimmer of hope; perhaps she could be the bridge to more concrete answers.

Excited by the prospect of helping me, Pam volunteered to reach out on my behalf. "I'll get in touch with Fred," she said enthusiastically. "I'm sure he'd be willing to talk to you." Her words gave me a renewed sense of hope. Pam's willingness to assist suggested that the answers I sought might be closer than ever. If Fred was as connected to the Barnett family as Pam described, he could possibly hold insights that would finally help me understand how Halimah, Lisa, and I were linked through our DNA.

So, with cautious optimism, I waited to connect with Fred Barnett, feeling that perhaps I was one step closer to uncovering the connections that had drawn me into this journey. Each new conversation, each new lead, was a step toward answers that could reshape everything I thought I knew about my family history. Shortly after my conversation with Pam, things moved quickly.

Fred Barnett, the man Pam had spoken of, was eager to connect, and soon, we arranged a time to talk. Because of COVID-19, our first conversation took place through a telephone conference. This setup allowed me not only to speak directly with Fred but also to connect with Lisa and one of Fred's daughters, who joined the call. The opportunity to converse with multiple family members at once created an immediate sense of inclusion – an invitation into a circle that, just months before, I hadn't even known existed.

Fred greeted me with warmth and enthusiasm. He was genuinely excited to connect, and as I listened, he began to share stories of the Barnett family. His words painted a vivid picture of cousins and connections, filling in gaps in the family tapestry that was previously unknown to me. Fred's eagerness to share and explore our connection gave me a profound sense of belonging. Each detail he recounted brought me a step closer to understanding my lineage, yet many questions remained unanswered.

As we pieced together family history, one crucial fact came to light: Fred was my second cousin. The realization was profound! This discovery confirmed that Fred was first cousins with my paternal biological origin – though, of course, neither of us knew yet which of the six Barnett brothers this could be. Each of these men, now part of my biological story, represented a potential paternal progenitor I had never known.

Fred, like me, had no way of knowing which of his six first cousins was my biological progenitor. The lack of certainty lingered, but the mystery carried with it a newfound sense of kinship, a connection that transcended the need for immediate answers. For now, it was enough to know that Fred was my family, that he, too, was on this journey of discovery alongside me. The call ended with a renewed commitment to continue our search, to uncover more about the Barnett brothers and the story that linked us together.

As we said our goodbyes, I was filled with gratitude and hope. Fred's openness, his willingness to share stories and memories, and his embrace of me and my family meant so much to me! Now, I had a family by my side – people who were as invested in this journey as I was. And to think Fred lives less than 30 minutes from me in the neighboring city of Cary... Wow! While the question of which Barnett brother was my biological progenitor remained unanswered, our shared connection was real and unwavering. We would move forward together, uncovering the legacy that connected us all.

During our conversation, Fred had shared that of the six Barnett brothers, he recalled that two of them, James and Leroy Barnett, had been stationed at Fort Bragg. This detail really caught my attention! According to Fred, James and Leroy would often stop by his home on their way back to New Jersey, giving me a glimpse into the travels and ties that bound the family across different states.

Fred also shared that James had passed away. He explained that James had eventually moved to Shelby, North Carolina, where he had a son and a daughter. Although I hadn't met them, hearing about James's children in Shelby made my connection to this family feel more tangible. These were people with whom I shared a lineage and perhaps even traits, yet whose lives had unfolded in ways separate from my own. The revelation was bittersweet, especially knowing that James had passed on, but still, it was another piece of my heritage falling into place. The thought that I might have siblings just two hours away was also exciting!

As we spoke, Fred had provided even more about the Barnett family's origins. He explained that the family originally hailed from Roxboro, North Carolina, and, around some 80 years ago, had migrated north to New Jersey. This journey from Roxboro to New Jersey was one of resilience, mirroring the broader migration patterns of many African American families seeking better opportunities. Their movement northward was a piece of family history that shaped not only my lineage but also the Barnett legacy in ways I was just beginning to understand.

These details deepened my appreciation for the story unfolding before me. Each new revelation brought me closer to understanding the lives of those who came before me, piecing together my own origins and the roots that linked me to this family I was just beginning to know. As Fred continued to share stories, the detail about Leroy and James being stationed at Fort Bragg, as I stated previously, gripped my attention like nothing else!

Out of the six Barnett brothers, my resemblance to Leroy and James stood out starkly in the photograph that I had received of the brothers. These similarities alone were striking, but there was more to consider. The fact that Leroy and James had both been stationed at Fort Bragg, located only about an hour and a half from Durham, North Carolina – where my mother lived seemed too significant to be a mere coincidence! This proximity added weight to my growing conviction that one of these two men might be my biological progenitor. It was as though the pieces of my family history, once scattered and obscured, were starting to form a coherent picture. Each revelation from my conversation with Fred had felt like a gentle push toward closure, drawing me closer to finally understanding the roots of my paternal lineage.

The excitement was undeniable. For the first time, I felt as though I was on the brink of discovering my biological identity. There was a thrill in knowing that I was closer than ever to unearthing the truth, to gaining the clarity I had sought for so long. The journey was far from over, but for the first time, I felt a solid sense of direction. I was no longer wandering through shadows of uncertainty; instead, I was piecing together a legacy – one that was uniquely mine, anchored in a lineage I had only recently discovered yet had always belonged to.

Reaching Out but Silence

Before initially communicating with Fred and after holding conversations with Halimah's mother, when Halimah initially reached out to me, I felt compelled to extend my search further. This journey toward discovering my paternal lineage had brought new names, faces, and family histories into my life, but there was still a missing piece. I needed concrete confirmation – something definitive that would clarify if I had siblings or close family among the Barnetts in New Jersey. So, I reached out to a few family members there. Resulting from my excitement, I thought it would be mutual. I'd hoped that these family members would be open to taking a DNA test to help confirm our connections.

I had the opportunity to speak with an aunt or two and even a couple of cousins or potential siblings. During our conversations, two of them initially expressed willingness to take the DNA test. Furthermore, not knowing anyone's financial situation, I offered to assist with the cost. I hoped their decision would be the breakthrough I needed to establish a clearer picture of my biological family ties. Unfortunately, despite their initial agreement, I never received confirmation that any of them had followed through with DNA testing. The silence was disappointing; each conversation had felt like a step forward, only to be halted by hesitation or uncertainty on their part.

The silence was puzzling to me, leaving me with unanswered questions and a lingering sense of incompleteness. It made absolutely no sense as to why there was silence and such reluctance to discover the truth about our Barnett family connections. And this being from both sides of my family members. I was on a journey that felt both close to and far from closure. I was left in a holding pattern, feeling the anticipation of discovery but also facing a measure of frustration. Yet, despite the setbacks, I remained optimistic and determined. This story, my story, was still unfolding, and I was committed to uncovering the truth. I believed that in due time, my *Daddy, the Difference Maker* and God would reveal my heart's desire to me.

There were two other Barnetts who expressed interest in taking the DNA test. From one of these individuals, there was never confirmation that they went through with the test. However, with the other Barnett family member, this entire DNA situation, along with the unknowns that this person wanted answers to, was troubling for them. I had the answers; however, I was sworn to secrecy. I strongly encouraged this person and ensured them that if they took the test, they would get answers to their questions. Sometime later this person came back as a match with me and the other Barnetts through DNA testing. Needless to say, they got their answers!

Though my conversations with Halimah had ended rather abruptly, her mother was considering taking a DNA test – not only in an attempt to trace her maternal lineage but to also confirm whether she and I were, in fact, siblings. The thought was thrilling. If Halimah's mother came back as my sister, it would serve as a key piece of this long, intricate puzzle, offering clarity on the identity of my biological father. The results would finally help bridge the gaps in my understanding of where I come from biologically, although there were questions about why I didn't have a DNA match with Halimah's uncle, who was believed to be her mother's brother.

It was only after I received photos of Halimah's grandfather I felt it was the right time to share my DNA discovery with my mother, hoping it might stir a memory, a connection, or recognition from her past that would help confirm my findings. This would begin an agonizing season for my mother; additionally, our relationship would become strained. My mother wasn't eager to embrace my discovery; nevertheless, I was not relenting.

When I showed her the picture, my mother looked briefly... too brief as far as I was concerned, and she responded that she did not recognize the man in the photograph. It was a small disappointment. However, my mother did point out family members that she immediately recognized from my DNA testing. Still, I found myself clinging to the hope that Halimah's mother's DNA test could provide the missing confirmation I sought.

As mentioned, I knew that bringing this DNA matter before my mother would be a difficult and emotionally charged road, but I was determined to pursue the truth. The questions swirling in my mind about my origins were relentless, and I was adamant about finding the answers – answers that could finally put the pieces of my identity together. However, my mother's response was not what I expected, and our path forward became even more complicated because she was and always had been reluctant to discuss her painful past.

When I showed her the picture of Halimah's grandfather, expecting perhaps a flicker of recognition or a connection to our past, I was met with her firm denial that she recognized him. As I stated, she looked at the photo briefly, and I said as much to her; I could see the reluctance in her eyes to look at the picture. And though her words were clear, I felt this was not just about the photo. There was more beneath the surface – a history and a set of emotions that I was not fully aware of. Growing up, I knew very little about my mother's past or upbringing. Nevertheless, our Daddy Dilemmas were now front and center!

This moment, as small as it may have seemed, was an emotional turning point! The distance between my mother and me widened with each attempt to push for answers regarding her past. It was me who took a step back. Because my mother didn't show eagerness to help me find answers, resulting from this, I was led to question her and some of her responses regarding her past. I had expected that we might find some common ground in this search and that the DNA results would bring us closer to understanding the family story we shared. Instead, I found myself walking a lonely road, pushing forward with questions that my mother seemed unwilling to answer. I say unwillingly, again, because my mother kept her past guarded or close to her.

It wasn't just the picture or the person in it; it was the deeper implications of my questions – the past that I was bringing to light, the stories of her painful past that had remained buried. However, to her, I was trying to unearth something that had no factual underpinning; oddly, she even questioned the validity or accuracy of DNA testing. To me, however, the need for truth was undeniable! As much as the path became difficult, I was determined to find not only my truth but also my son's truth. My search became his truth and our truth for perhaps generations to come! I needed to know where we came from and who we truly were!

With each turn in this journey, I was learning not only about my family's history but also about the complexities of relationships, memory, and denial. This wasn't just about DNA. It was about understanding the choices that shaped our lives, the secrets that were kept, and the truths that were still waiting to be revealed. The struggle to understand my past was becoming a deeply personal one for those closely connected to this Daddy Dilemma, but it was a road I had to walk, even if it meant walking it without the help of my mother and family.

As I continued the search for answers, I found myself speaking more with Halimah's mother. The more I learned, the more I felt a connection to her family, even though there were still so many unanswered questions. It was during one of our later conversations that I shared the DNA connection between Halimah, Lisa Barnett, and me. I explained how Halimah and I were connected through our DNA and how Lisa Barnett also appeared as a shared match for both Halimah and me.

When I mentioned Lisa and the Barnett family, Halimah's mother didn't acknowledge knowing or having any connection to this family at all. This was another one of those frustrating moments in this search. Each time I thought I was getting closer to the truth, there was another piece of the puzzle that didn't seem to fit. Halimah's mother eventually took the next step... her DNA testing. If nothing else, I could sense that she wanted to know the truth as much as I did, though her approach to it was more cautious. She seemed to hold her cards close to her chest, reluctant to admit more than she was ready to reveal. Nonetheless, she submitted her DNA test, a significant step toward uncovering the truth.

Sometime during the early months of 2022, Halimah's mother sent in her DNA sample. At this point, I had already come to realize that this journey of discovery wasn't going to be a straightforward one. But still, I held onto hope. Perhaps this test would provide the clarity I was searching for. I knew that with every test submitted and every conversation I had, I was getting closer to discovering my truth. The search for my true identity, my biological progenitor, and the intricate web of family ties was complicated, but I couldn't give up now. With Halimah's mother's test submitted, I knew it was just a matter of time before the next chapter of this journey would unfold.

A Revelation Unveiled

The DNA results for Halimah's mother arrived in the spring – April 7th, 2022 (ironically, a time of renewal), but unfortunately, they did not provide the results I had hoped for. Despite the undeniable DNA connection I shared with Halimah, her mother did not come back as a match; Halimah's mother was not my sister. This came as quite a surprise to me. Based on the initial information that Halimah provided to me. How could Halimah and I share a match, but her mother and I did not? I was left scratching my head, trying to make sense of things.

Our conversation about the results was brief and somewhat uneventful. Halimah's mother didn't seem to be as concerned about the discrepancies as I was, but I could sense she was trying to make sense of the situation. We made small talk about the results, and the conversation seemed to be winding down. But just before we ended our conversation, she said something that would change the trajectory of this entire journey.

With a tone that was reluctant and cautious, as though she knew this would be difficult to admit, Halimah's mother finally shared something quite significant. She said, "When you first mentioned the name Lisa Barnett (which was weeks earlier), I had a nightmare." It was actually a shocking revelation that was brought to her and a significant Daddy Dilemma! I listened intently with eager anticipation! She explained that she had dated one of the Barnett brothers, Roger Barnett. They had been in a relationship for a time, but ultimately, they had stopped dating. She had entered into a relationship with another man. As far as Halimah's mother was concerned when she realized that she was pregnant, she believed this other man to be the father of her child. Everything started to fall into place.

Halimah's mother had not just recognized the name "Barnett" it was connected to her past in a much more profound way than she had initially considered. The revelation that she had dated Roger Barnett was the missing link. Now, everything began to make sense. I could tell this was a hard pill for her to swallow. After all these years, she had to confront the reality that the man she had believed to be Halimah's father for 43 years was not actually her daughter's biological father. And for Halimah, the same truth would soon come to light – that the man she had called her father was not her biological father after all. This was an incredibly difficult and complex truth to accept, and it would no doubt take time for them to process and heal from. What a Daddy Dilemma! What potential Mama Drama they now faced!

Though the reality was clear to me, I knew that this was no longer my journey to navigate with them. We had uncovered the truth, but this was something Halimah and her mother would have to work through on their own. I wasn't part of this family's history in the way I had originally thought. But in uncovering this major piece of our life's puzzle, I had played a role in helping them begin the process of understanding who they truly were, at least for Halimah, although I'm inclined to believe that she saw the potential of her story unfolding in such a way early on.

A New Understanding

The revelation about my connection to Halimah and Lisa Barnett through the paternal lineage of the Barnett family helped me make sense of so many unanswered questions. The pieces of the puzzle that had been scattered for so long began to fall into place. It was a relief, yet at the same time, it was an unsettling truth for some. But the clarity it provided about my identity was undeniable – biologically, I was a Barnett. My story, which had been so fragmented, was finally taking shape in a way that felt real, as a different chapter was now emerging through my DNA journey to my paternal progenitor.

With this newfound understanding, it was now time to reengage with my mother to share the truth and new discovery with her – no longer just a hint but a firm belief. For reasons not fully disclosed here, I'd chosen to distance myself from my mother. Now, I had to tell her that the individual in the picture, the person who I had so strongly resembled, was not my biological progenitor after all. I had once convincingly thought that Halimah's grandfather was the man who had fathered me, but now it was clear that he was not. It was now clear that my true paternal lineage was connected to the Barnett family.

I didn't think it would be an easy conversation, but I knew it was necessary. I carefully shared with my mother, who was more receptive to hearing from me than in previous times, that, paternally, I was certain I was a Barnett. I explained how my connection with Halimah and Lisa Barnett as a result of Halimah's mother's disclosure certainly pointed me to this conclusion. While it wasn't the answer I had initially expected, it was the one that was true. My mother listened quietly and receptively as I explained the situation.

I could see the weight of the truth settling in on her face, but she didn't respond immediately. It wasn't easy for her to hear that the man (Linwood Bullock) she had believed to be my father was not, in fact, my biological parent. But there was no denying the evidence. And as difficult as it was for her, this was the truth that had been uncovered. The Barnett family was my true paternal heritage, and the story of my origins was becoming clearer with the passing of time.

It was a bittersweet moment. The person I had thought was my biological father (Linwood, although I'd always said I didn't resemble him) and the family I had been connected to for so long were no longer the truth of my lineage. Yet, at the same time, I felt a sense of peace in knowing that my biological identity was now being restored through the discovery of the Barnett connection. I will add. Although I didn't resemble Linwood, I never thought once that he wasn't my biological father. I had no reason to question what I'd been told. Neither did he ever suggest or hint to me otherwise. As a matter of fact, Linwood would address me as – "Son."

I wasn't sure where the road ahead would lead, but now, at least, I had a clearer understanding of my past and a stronger sense of who I was biologically.

CHAPTER 7

A Mother's Nightmare!

Aday or two after I had shared with my mother the revelation regarding the Barnett connection, she stated her need to talk to me. This time, my mother's demeanor was different – somewhat subdued. When we met together, she looked as though she had something heavy on her mind, something unsettling to say. It was clear that the conversation we'd had had lingered in her thoughts, but I wasn't expecting what she was about to tell me.

"Son," she began softly, "I had a nightmare. A literal nightmare!"

Her voice was resolute and she was seriously focused as she spoke, and I could tell this wasn't just a passing thought – it was something that had deeply affected her! She went on,

"I woke up horrified!" She continued, "I couldn't recall anything specific about the dream, but there was this one thing; the name – Barnett! Barnett! Barnett! It kept echoing loudly in my mind!"

I listened intently, waiting to hear more about what she had to say. The lineage and name Barnett had been the key piece of information that had started this entire journey with Halimah and, ultimately, Lisa Barnett.

However, the name Barnett, my mother heard for the first time a day or two earlier. Hearing my mother speak of the name with such distress had claimed my full attention! I could see the fear and confusion in her eyes as she relayed the imageless nightmare to me, and I knew this was no ordinary dream. I am convinced that *Dad, our Difference Maker*, had shown up to make a difference, to bring an end to my search for truth!

My mother went on to explain how, as she sat up in bed shaken from the nightmare, the name Barnett was stuck in her mind. It was as if the name was somehow forcing its way into her thoughts, like a persistent calling out to her that she couldn't ignore. My mother said that she began to ponder and try to figure out why the name "Barnett" resounded and haunted her in such a way! The name Barnett wasn't just a coincidence; it was a trigger – something tied to a part of her past that she had forgotten and buried deep within as she was accustomed and forced to do as a fatherless and motherless child and even as a young adult.

Resulting from her nightmare, her subconscious had brought to the surface trauma she had long buried in an attempt to maintain her sanity and to survive. The name Barnett was no longer just a piece of the puzzle; it was a key to unlocking a deeper truth! As I listened to my mother's recounting of her pictureless nightmare, I knew that her past was coming forward in ways she wasn't prepared for. She said that as she tried to recall the name Barnett, her thoughts drifted to a place and time in her life – New Jersey and New York.

My mother was forced to work odd jobs and find work wherever she could. This led to her dropping out of high school. Later, she would get her G.E.D., and as a mother, she also went to night school and became a Licensed Practical Nurse (LPN). Beforehand, my mother worked odd jobs, tending to the homes of white people, keeping their kids, and doing whatever she could to make ends meet. My mother continued, "I remember standing at a bus stop in New Jersey when a man pulled up. He asked if I needed a ride. He didn't look threatening, so I accepted."

She described the brief interaction with him, recalling how they exchanged small talk as he drove. My mother stated, "He mentioned that he had family in either Raleigh or Durham," however, she wasn't certain where. She continued, "He stopped at a store or somewhere while I remained in the car. After that, he took me to my destination, and that was the last time I saw him."

During this time, my mother was quite young, just around 20 years old. Now, at the age of 79, she shared with me that as she attempted to recall her past, her thoughts took her back to when she once lived in a boarding house in Durham, located at 1406 Fayetteville Street. The day following her nightmare, she stated that she gave thought to her past. She said that she was led to drive to the abandoned boarding house; it had been owned and operated by a woman named Mrs. Michaux.

My mother spoke of her with a level of respect. She remembered Mrs. Michaux as someone who ran a "tight ship," someone who didn't "tolerate nonsense." My mother said to me, "I remember that Mrs. Michaux came to me and said some guy had arrived to see me. It was at night; therefore, he was not permitted to enter. I went to see who it was. When I went outside, I couldn't believe my eyes. It was him! The man who gave me a ride when I was in New Jersey."

"How did you find me… what do you want… why are you hear?" My mother stated she asked him. My mother had not sought him out, and he had not given her any indication that he would come looking for her. Yet there he was, standing at her door that night. My mother didn't offer any details, neither did I ask. She simply stated, "That's when it happened." After that, she went silent. She stared at me with pleading and painful eyes! After a moment of silence, I asked my mother, "Did he rape you?" With a hesitant and slow head nod, she acknowledged, "Yes."

After making this acknowledgment, my mother, looking into my eyes, responded, "Son, I've gone through worse!" I remember thinking, "Worse?!" And then given thought to what she must have had to endure as a fatherless and motherless child!

I could see the heaviness in her eyes – the weight of a past she had buried so deep, so far out of reach, that even bringing it up again seemed like a betrayal to her own sense of survival. The emotional toll of that moment was overwhelming. What could I say? What could I possibly understand about the depth of her pain? She had opened up about something monumental, something she had long suppressed in her memory for almost 6 decades.

I didn't ask her about what she meant by "worse." I didn't need to. Whatever it was, it was too heavy for words. But in that instant, I knew more than I had ever known before about my mother's struggles and the dilemmas she faced! She had lived and survived through hellish things I could never have imagined! And by the grace of God, her *Dad and Difference Maker,* against all odds, she was given the strength to persevere! She had lived her life, fought her battles, and protected me and my siblings from things I would never have comprehended as a child; such things she worked hard to defend her children against!

I then realized that my mother's story was far from simple. It was filled with complexities, with truths that had been hidden for decades, and with a past that had shaped her in ways I could never have known. All of this because of Daddy Dilemmas! My mother was now left to grapple with painful realities that she had long suppressed, such horrors she had learned to bury deep within herself as a child growing up without a father and mother.

Her life had been filled with hardship, and no doubt, she had been taken advantage of in ways unfathomable and beyond belief! I could only imagine the weight of the emotions she was dealing with now, especially as my mother had to confront the painful truth about how the son she unquestionably loved had actually been conceived – through sexual assault and not by Linwood, who she was dating when she realized she was pregnant.

It must have been a crushing revelation for her, and I could see it in her eyes as she processed revealing our truth. This was not just about her own past but about what had happened to her and how it had shaped my own existence. I hurt with her at that moment! Someone had hurt my mother, and no matter how much time had passed, the pain of that truth had never fully gone away for her; now, the ripple effect had come my way! As for the revelation of my conception, this didn't trouble me, not in the least. By the grace and mercy of God, I now had a calm and closer closure to my search for my paternal progenitor.

The revelation about my paternal lineage – being a Barnett, finally gave me something I had been searching for, a nearing – closure! Even without knowing this subordinate biological reality of mine, as a child of God, I was confident in my eternal identity and reality and who I'd become because I belonged to God – my *Daddy, the Ultimate Difference Maker! I WAS HIS SON – HE IS MY DADDY!* **His love for me is and always has been unquestionable! In the end, this is all that truly matters!**

Going back in time to my first introduction to my Barnett family upstate. Over the next year and a half or so, and prior to my mother's nightmare. I had a couple of brief conversations with my Barnett family members, but nothing substantial came from them. Despite my hopes, there was no real cooperation or willingness from anyone to take the DNA test. My communication with them dwindled as quickly as it was initiated, and I moved forward, still holding onto the hope that one day, the answer I was searching for regarding who actually was my paternal progenitor would come. I'd even added the name Barnett to my social media accounts to perhaps help facilitate this process.

Then, in June of 2024, something unexpected happened! I received a Facebook friend request from a young lady named Laray Glover Leach. I saw that we had Barnett friends in common, which intrigued me; I decided to accept her friend request, curious to see what connection might be there. After connecting with Laray through Facebook, our conversation quickly moved to communicating directly through talks over the phone.

She shared with me an interesting tidbit from a casual chat she'd had with her brother. She said, he nonchalantly mentioned to her, "By the way, you know you possibly have another brother?" He was one of the Barnett family members that I'd spoken to previously. Surprised by this revelation, she was somewhat disappointed to learn that it had taken so long for anyone to tell her about me – "about two years," she stated. There was a sense of regret or disappointment in her voice that "time had been lost," and this information had not been shared with her.

Despite the initial shock and revelation about me, Laray immediately embraced the idea of having me as a brother or cousin. Her enthusiasm and openness were palpable. She was genuinely excited, eager to know if we were truly siblings. The conversation we had couldn't have gone better. In fact, she was so eager to confirm our potential sibling connection that the very next day, she ordered a DNA test. She said something quite funny to me; as we talked, she said, "I will be a good sister."

Over the following month or so, the anticipation for her results was mutual. We both eagerly awaited the outcome, communicating daily, hopeful that the DNA test would confirm that we were siblings, though we also knew the possibility that we could be first cousins. Nevertheless, we both hoped that the test would reveal the truth we'd been waiting for, that we were indeed siblings. I specifically and passionately prayed, informing my *Daddy* that I wanted this to be the outcome; "I wanted Laray to be my sister!" There's only been a few times that I've prayed with such specificity. And God, even Laray, knew why.

On July 11th, 2024, shortly after Laray submitted her DNA kit, the test results arrived. Unbeknownst to me, that night, Laray had sent me a text message revealing that we were first cousins. I'll admit I was disappointed when I saw this! However, upon reviewing the test results that morning on my Ancestry account, I immediately recognized the *Centimorgan number of 1,781* and the way she showed up on my ancestry list – as my half-sister, that her Dad, James Barnett, was, in fact, my paternal progenitor! Finally, the journey of discovery that I had been on for so long (5 years) had come to a close!

I gave Laray a call and explained the actual results to her; she was then surprised and thrilled! Her enthusiasm matched mine as we both celebrated the fact that we had connected. And that my quest was now over! We were now family, not just in name but through the bond of shared DNA from the dad she loved, James, and my newly discovered paternal progenitor. In addition to Laray being my sibling, she informed me that there are two other brothers – one living in Pennsylvania and another in Mount Holly, North Carolina. There is also a potential third brother who might be somewhere in Georgia, though his whereabouts remain unknown. While we have yet to find him, I remain hopeful that, in time, we will connect with him as well.

As I reflect on the journey of discovery that has unfolded before me, I am reminded of the stark contrast between fathers – a Dad the Difference Maker and a Dad the Dilemma – and how these roles have shaped and affected positively as well as negatively not only my life but also the lives of those around me. As well… countless others whose stories will never be told or made known!

Through what's been shared in this book, we see both the struggles because of Dad the Dilemma – the pain, confusion, and brokenness that can arise from the choices of a man who rejects his responsibility. Or who willfully or otherwise does not have God as his *Difference Maker*. Contrasting, Dad the Difference Maker – a godly man who has committed his life to image Jesus, his Lord and Savior – *The Ultimate Difference Maker*.

In Dad a Difference Maker, there is that godly husband and dad or man who strives to live his life and purpose according to God's will. Such a man's life becomes a beacon of hope and light for others, a reflection of the love, guidance, and leadership that our Heavenly Father provides. It is this kind of man and fatherhood – one built on integrity, faith, and a deep connection to the will of God – that shapes families, strengthens communities, and creates lasting legacies.

Conversely, Dad the Dilemma is a man who, whether through ignorance or defiance, fails to embrace his calling to lead with love and responsibility. His choices bring division, pain, and hardship, not just for himself but for everyone under his care. He is the one who sows seeds of confusion and leaves a trail of hurt. Yet, even in the face of such brokenness, there is the possibility of redemption, for God's grace is greater than any dilemma we face!

In closing this chapter, I am left with a deep conviction: fatherhood is not just a biological role; it is a divine calling with eternal consequences! And as we walk through this life, whether as sons or as fathers, we are called as men to choose which legacy we will embrace – the legacy of Dad the Difference Maker, who reflects the love and leadership of our Heavenly Father, or the legacy of Dad the Dilemma, whose actions reflect the brokenness and consequences of rejecting God's will. It is through our choices that we shape the future – not just for ourselves but for the generations to come, even so, one's eternal state. May you choose wisely!

As I continue to embrace my new role as a grandfather and as a man striving to follow Christ, I am reminded of the importance of making a difference in the lives of everyone who enters my sphere of influence. The journey of discovery – of understanding my own family, my identity, and the power of Biblical Manhood – has taught me that the most significant thing I can do is to be a Difference Maker in the lives of those who are providentially or divinely brought my way.

The Full Circle of Discovery

This journey of discovery. From my first conversations with Halimah and her mother to the unexpected connections with Laray and everyone else involved, these unveilings have reminded me not only about my own identity but also about the transformative power of connection, grace, and redemption!

The impact of a dad – whether earthly or heavenly – is immeasurable! As I continue to reflect on these revelations, I am reminded that our identity is not just defined by our past or our family but by our relationship with the Father in Heaven! Through Him, we find our *true identity*, healing, and purpose! As we move forward, we should carry with us the lessons of this life's journey: that the difference between life and death, healing and brokenness, comes down to the *Father* (or father) we choose to follow. As for me, I am determined to continue to follow my *Daddy, the Ultimate Difference Maker*, God, who restores, redeems, and guides us toward the fullness of life; the God and Daddy who calls me beloved – and His son! That's who I am! I am a child of God – His son!… nothing else, no matter the circumstances that brought us into this world, matters! If you have accepted Jesus as your Lord and Savior, you are, in fact, our *Daddy's* sons and daughters! **Period! And Amen!**

The Barnett Family's Story and the Impact of Fatherlessness

With the limited information that I've been able to glean regarding my Barnett lineage, I've attempted and continue to convey a mere fraction of their journey and story. I pray that I've represented them accurately. As part of my journey to understand my heritage, I uncovered the story of the Barnett family's move north to New Jersey from Roxboro, N.C. In this move, James, my paternal progenitor's – parents, and their ten (?) children – relocated with the hope of a better life. Among the children were six boys and four girls, each close in age. Tragically, at a young age, these siblings lost both their mother (Georgia William Barnett) and father (James Ollie Barnett), who were merely in their *thirties* and *forties* when they passed, leaving their children without parental guidance during some of their most formative years.

With the loss of their parents, it was left to other family members and one or two of the older sisters to help care for the younger siblings as best they could. These older siblings, already facing the hardship of loss, stepped in to do what they could to provide support and guidance. Yet, without the foundational presence of a father to guide, protect, and mentor them, the six boys, in particular, no doubt, faced significant dilemmas! Boys especially need a father to model strong character, enforce discipline, and provide a clear direction in life.

The absence of a father in the lives of these young men (and sisters) no doubt led to understandable struggles! Without the strong presence of a dad to steer them away from missteps and toward the right path had to affect each of these children. Regarding these boys specifically, I merely speculate that they had no sustainable, reliable, and consistent father figure to correct, instruct, or help them make decisions that would honor God and lead them toward a life of responsibility and integrity when they were young men.

Such a void, even a hole in their soul, often leaves boys vulnerable, making it more likely for them to grow up with struggles and unresolved challenges or, as I term it in this book, even becoming Daddy Dilemmas.

Presumably, these boys, maturing in age to become young men who, without a godly father's influence, struggle with identity, direction, and discipline, being challenged to offer to their offspring that which they lacked because of life's dilemmas that they encountered and which were beyond their control.

Reflecting on their most likely and reasonably accepted story, I recognize that the struggles they faced were not unique. I, too, understand the void left by the absence of a father. Growing up without a dad, I faced challenges that I often met without the necessary wisdom, protection, or guidance that only a father can provide. My own journey, especially from my early teens into young adulthood, had its share of dilemmas and/or life lessons, many of which could have been avoided had I received the fatherly support and direction I so needed from Dad, a Difference Maker.

My challenges or dilemmas could have proved to be rather costly, with some choices I made potentially being far more damaging and/or consequential than I even realized at the time. But then I began to mature as a godly man – yes, I grew up! I would like to believe that this was the case for my Barnett uncles, who are now deceased. And I know this was the case for James Barnett Jr., aka Juni, so stated Laray of my paternal progenitor, who passed away in 2008. In a conversation that I had with Laray, she felt confident in sharing the following, she stated, "If my Dad was alive, he would apologize to you and would want to also apologize to your mother. I have every reason to believe this would have been the case. And I would have embraced his apology without holding his past against him.

In acknowledging this, I find forgiveness and grace – not only for myself but for the Barnett men and even my paternal progenitor. The legacy of fatherlessness can be a heavy burden to carry, yet I believe that understanding this weight allows us to confront it with compassion. Rather than holding the wrong steps or poor choices made by those without a father against them, I recognize these dilemmas as part of a larger narrative of brokenness that only *God, The Ultimate Difference Maker*, our Heavenly Father, can truly restore and reconcile back to Himself.

Stop the Presses!

Literally, the presses were stopped – my publishing process halted! On November 27, 2024, I had submitted this book for publishing. Just over a month later, on January 10, 2025, I received an email from my publisher indicating that my book was awaiting my final approval for printing and distribution. However, before I received this email notification, earlier in the day, at approximately 9 am., an unexpected event arose that further unfolded my DNA story! I discovered that I have another brother, his name is John Minor, Sr.

As I mentioned previously, in the spring of 2024, my then-unknown sister, Laray, reached out to me via Facebook. However, after receiving her DNA test results just over a month later, it was then confirmed that she was my sister. Laray also revealed to me at that time that I had three other brothers. Since this recent turn of events, she's added that there may also be another sister, Valerie Banks, who is believed to reside in South Carolina.

And so it was for me, to say the least, quite a surprise on that morning of Friday, January 10, 2025, at 8:39 and also 8:57 a.m., that I received an Ancestry message and notification via Ancestry and another Facebook message from John Minor Sr., which read,

"Greetings, My Name is John Miner I am 51 years old. I am originally from Plainfield NJ I now reside in Davenport FL. I was raised by my mom Toni and was adopted by my step father Ed Miner. I never knew who my biological father was but I heard many rumors that his last name was Barnett. I've always wondered if I had any other family members out there, but was reluctant because I didn't want to up *(open?)* any closed closets. I've never done research until now due to my wife gifting me the Ancestry.com DNA test for Christmas. This morning I received my results and noticed that you and I shared 23% DNA and stating that you could be my half-brother or uncle. I know that this could be a shock however, if you are willing I would love to talk to you and see if we are truly related. I've looked you up on Facebook and seen that you are a man of God and we resemble one another. If you would like to talk my telephone number is 813-xxx-xxxx."

It was this very morning as mentioned, that John received his Ancestry test results that he had been anxiously waiting for each day since he submitted his DNA for testing, which ultimately connected him and me as relatives. After verifying John's results through my Ancestry account, I immediately recognized that we were, in fact, brothers – that he also was biologically a Barnett. Anticipating his excitement and eagerness to hear from me, I promptly gave him a call. John was tearfully glad that I responded to him!

For the remainder of the day, we talked off and on. I provided him with my DNA journey and story, and he provided me with his life's story as well. I then began to piece together for him our biological connection, portions of which or people he had years or decades prior known or interacted with. He, along with his mother, who he later talked to, filled in the remaining pieces that unquestionably and relationally actually reconnected John to the Barnetts. After talking to his mother, John discovered that his story and mine, unfortunately, were quite similar.

John was able to discover within a matter of hours his complete story via his DNA testing and his talk with me and his mother. Whereas with me, my journey stretched over 4 ½ years, with this new discovery of John being my brother totaling 5 years, 1 month and just under 2 weeks. It was for this reason I was able to say to John, "It's great that we have made this discovery that we are brothers. However, I am more happy for him and his family because he finally had closure and paternal identity." This was something John stated to me that had haunted and troubled him for his life-time! What a Daddy Dilemma!

CHAPTER 8

A Picture of Dad, a Difference Maker

As I approach the conclusion of this book, I want to leave a foundational truth with my sons (their children), my readers, and all fathers who aspire to be Difference Makers within your sphere of influence or within your families: no person or dad, including me, has ever functioned perfectly in the role of husband or father or other. I've shared that I stumbled, failed, and made mistakes along the way, often failing to meet the standards I set for myself as a follower or disciple of Jesus.

The imperfection of fathers (mankind) can be traced back to the effects of sin, which corrupts every area of human life. Sin, remaining in our mortal and corrupt bodies, hinders even our best intentions. Yet, perfection is not the standard God requires of us. He requires holiness or righteousness, which is found only by walking in His will and being led by His Spirit. That said, we are still held accountable for missing the mark. We can't just excuse or wink at our sinful failures. We are to feel regret for our shortcomings but not condemnation (Romans 8:1). After acknowledging our errors before God and asking for forgiveness we then move forward in life as we continue to resist or do battle against our sinful nature.

As Scripture says, *"The righteous man walks in his integrity; his children are blessed after him"* (Proverbs 20:7). Though we fall short, when we seek

God's righteousness and walk in integrity, our children will reap the blessings. Where I got it right, where I chose to function righteously, I know that the impact was meaningful to my family and those under my influence. Perfection will always elude us, but faithfulness and a heart committed to God's ways can leave a legacy that outlasts our failures.

The Role of Dad: Cheerleader and Coach

A father's role in his children's lives requires a balance of love and discipline. On the one hand, dads are called to be their children's biggest cheerleaders – motivating, encouraging, and celebrating their efforts! On the other hand, dads must also take on the role of a coach – teaching, correcting, and equipping their children for the challenges of life.

"Fathers, do not provoke your children to anger, but bring them up in the discipline and instruction of the Lord" (Ephesians 6:4). This verse encapsulates the delicate balance of discipline and love that a father must maintain.

Cal Scott came into my life when I was a mere babe – not yet a toddler. He then divorced himself from our family when I was around 11 years of age. When I needed him most – he was gone! And so, I didn't have a father to model these roles for me. My dad wasn't there to cheer me on, coach me, or show me the way. His absence left a void that shaped my understanding of what I wanted to give my sons. I didn't want them to grow up without support, without guidance, or without the reassurance of a father who believed in them.

The joy and job of parenting: For years, I dedicated myself to being both cheerleader and coach for my sons. I took my youngest son to football camps, football combines, and training sessions, both near and far, with both sons participating in soccer, track, baseball, and other activities. I worked tirelessly, with my wife's assistance, to support our sons. As for my youngest he received more involved training by me to support his dream of playing at a higher level, training him and preparing him for the opportunities ahead. And so, it wasn't just about football; it was about instilling discipline, perseverance, and the drive to excel.

Those efforts paid off when my son received collegiate scholarship offers from schools across the state and beyond. Ultimately, he accepted a full-ride football scholarship to Duke University. But what also mattered was not only this accomplishment but the character he demonstrated along the way. As for my oldest son, he's been excelling as a United States Marine for the past two decades. Considering my upbringing… Yes, I pat myself on the back and thank God – my *Help!*

Father and Son: Partners, Not Competitors

A father's role in his maturing or adult son's life is never one of competition unless it's in having fun. The father does not measure his success against that of his son, and neither should the son see himself in competition with his father. Instead, they are partners, walking a path where the father leads, guides, and cheers his son onward to be the best that he can be. When this is done, the entire family benefits short and long-term!

As for girl dads, teach your daughters about the trappings of godless boys; make sure your daughters know their worth as a child of God. Also, teach them to be self-sufficient as they rely on God. Dads, if you lead well, your wife will lovingly submit well. Both your sons and daughters must see how well you two operate as a team; in this, you are modeling the Triune God… God the Father, Son, and Holy Spirit (John 6:38 & 14:28; 1 Corinthians 11:3 &15:28).

"Like arrows in the hand of a warrior, so are the children of one's youth" (Psalm 127:4). Fathers launch their children into the world, not to compete with them but to guide them toward hitting their mark. Again, when this is done, the family as a whole benefits!

While there is no competition, there is a deep desire in the heart of every good father to see his children at least match, if not exceed, his own accomplishments. Where the father has succeeded in maintaining his home, being respectful to his wife, and providing the necessities of life for his children, he wants his sons to reach the same standard – or go beyond it.

But the ultimate goal is not competition or even comparison. It is about enabling the son or daughter to build a quality life for himself or herself and their family – a life where they do not have to endure unnecessary struggles caused by poor decisions or avoidable missteps. This is not about pride or ego; it is about love. A father who has walked the path of life knows its challenges and wants to clear the way for his offspring to walk it with greater ease and success. We live in an ever-changing and uncertain world! I don't want you to think that I'm measuring success by what your child accomplishes or acquires. In all they are attempting to get, they must first get God! Having Him is the measure of true success and greatness (Proverbs 4:7; Ecclesiastes 12:13; Philippians 3:7,8)!

Two Sons, One Dad

In raising my two sons – Desmond and Mario, I have seen the fruits of God's grace in unique ways. Desmond is my biological child, while Mario is my child through marriage. Though not my biological son, I never referred to him as my stepson. He was my son, and I sought to raise him as such – with all the love, discipline, and provision I could offer. For different reasons, this was easier said than done. More is shared about this matter in my first book.

Raising a son when he has a biological father in his life can create its own unique challenges for all involved. I had to work at overcoming mine; it would seem that I did. My wife and Mario have acknowledged that I did well as a dad; even Mario's biological father thanked me for a job well done upon Mario's graduating from high school. Nevertheless, the Daddy Dilemma before me was ever-present. I must say I gave no thought to navigating the delicate balance of being a dad in my home while respecting the relationship that Mario had with his biological father. I simply parented my son according to the principles and values that I set for my household, even though things may have worked differently with Mario's biological dad. At the time, I couldn't even consider what a dilemma this must have been for Mario.

I'll admit, I didn't grasp the challenges and dilemmas this created for him. Having to follow my lead, my discipline, and my guidance may not have been easy for him. Yet, despite these challenges, from my observation, Mario has fared well. Although, without him discussing the details, he's recently made me aware of what I can describe as his Daddy Dilemmas, I am assuming as a result of what is being discussed through this book and what's being said now. Again, he seems to be doing well. Even so, I pray more for my sons and their families than ever before!

After graduating from high school, Mario went on to join the military – the Marines, where he still serves with distinction 22 years later. He is soon to be promoted to Sergeant Major and will be retiring from the Marines in three years with distinctions and honorable service. He has achieved the highest levels of leadership within his field. He is also a father – a "girl dad" who has done an extraordinary job raising his daughter and building a stable and comfortable life for his family. His accomplishments and character are a testament to God's faithfulness and the hard work he has put into his life.

I will add, in addition to raising Mario to become a self-sufficient man and solid Marine. Before he went off to the Marines, I took him to the Durham Police Department's shooting range, where I taught him how to shoot firearms. Additionally, I instructed him on other military disciplines that would prepare him for this journey. I remember the pride and accomplishment I felt when Mario thanked me. Either in a letter or phone call, Mario expressed his gratitude for how I raised and prepared him for this chapter in his life. He mentioned how he had to teach his fella Marines how to tie their ties and shine their footwear. If my memory is correct, and I think it is, Mario was appointed a leader over his Marine brothers while they were going through basic training.

As for my biological son, he, too, has flourished. Married with a son of his own, he has built a life that exceeds even my highest expectations. As a business owner, he has taken the lessons I taught him – about discipline, integrity, and perseverance, and applied them to his own journey. Like his brother, he has excelled, becoming not just a successful man but a godly husband and father.

Both of my sons have met and exceeded my expectations, and for this, I am profoundly grateful to God! My continued prayer along with my wife, is for them to be the Difference Makers or godly men that God has purposed them to be. *"Behold, children are a heritage from the Lord, the fruit of the womb a reward"* (Psalm 127:3). Their success is not just theirs but a reflection of God's blessings as I attempted to be the best godly Dad and Difference Maker that I knew to be when they were under my care and guidance.

Always a Dad, Always a Coach

While I haven't coached in years, there are still those who call me Coach, a few who, out of respect and endearment, will call me Dad, perhaps Pops, and even "Unc." As for "Coach," it's a title that has stayed with me, a reminder of the role I once played and the impact I made in the lives of others. In the same way, a father is always a father, even when his children are grown and building families of their own. Yet, one of the challenges of fatherhood is learning when to step back and not overstep our boundaries. As fathers, we must recognize that our role evolves over time. Adult children listen: While we are no longer actively coaching or parenting in the same way, our concern for our children's well-being never fades.

Therefore, *"Listen to your father, who gave you life, and do not despise your mother when she is old"* (Proverbs 23:22). Adult children, it's important to understand this: when your father or mother offers advice, it's not because they want to control your life or run your household. It's because they care deeply about your well-being, your family, and your future.

Therefore, hear them out and welcome your parents' opinions, values, and wisdom. Be glad that you still have a father or mother in your life to offer you their knowledge and guidance. This is not an intrusion; it's love. It's the heart of a parent who wants nothing but the best for you! Parents, make sure to stay in your lane. Be sure to talk to one another to ensure that mutual respect for boundaries is maintained with your adult children. Adult children, remember to be respectful to your parents at all times!

Though I failed and had fallen short at times, as a dad, my ultimate goal has always been to be a reflection or imager of our heavenly Father. *"Be imitators of God, as beloved children"* (Ephesians 5:1). I have sought to model my life after Jesus as a godly man, knowing that He is the *Ultimate Daddy and Difference Maker*. If we do this, He is well pleased. We will not do things perfectly, but we can surely do things right or righteously (Philippians 4:13).

The Eternal Victory

As I reflect on my journey as a father, I am reminded that the greatest victory is not found in this life but in the life to come! This world, with all its successes and failures, will one day pass away. But for those who remain in Christ, there is an eternal hope that cannot be shaken!

"But thanks be to God, who gives us the victory through our Lord Jesus Christ" (1 Corinthians 15:57).

Closing Thoughts And Benediction

To my sons, I say this. You've heard this from me before: "Be better fathers than I was. Not only take your children to church. Teach them early to know God as their *True Dad and Difference Maker*. Encourage them to distinguish between the fairy tales and lies of this world and the eternal truth of who God is."

And to all, but most importantly, fathers, I leave you with this challenge: Look to God, the *Ultimate Dad* and the *True Difference Maker*, as your guide and example. Love your families well, lead with integrity, and point your children to Christ. In the end, the greatest legacy you can leave is one that reflects the heart of the Father – Jehovah!

As this journey comes to a close, may the truths and reflections within these pages inspire fathers, sons, families, and all to pursue the heart of the *Ultimate Difference Maker – our* heavenly *Dad.* To my sons and all who read this work, remember this: God has called each of us to be more than mere seed bearers, and mothers, incubators; He has called us to be stewards, protectors, and leaders who reflect His love, His discipline, and His righteousness.

The role of a father, whether biological or not, carries the power to shape generations! It is not a burden to bear lightly but a divine commission that demands our utmost humility, integrity, and faithfulness. Even in our imperfections, God's grace is sufficient to transform our failures into testimonies and our efforts into legacies.

To my sons, to fathers everywhere, and to every child seeking to know the heart of the Father: Be mindful of the choices before you every day. Will you be a Difference Maker, one who aligns with the will of God and leads others toward Him? Or will you remain or become a Dilemma, contributing to the brokenness that sin brings into this world?

May you always look to the One who is both Father and Redeemer – the God who heals our wounds, restores our brokenness, and equips us to leave a lasting impact on those we love. As the Psalmist reminds us, *"As for me and my house, we will serve the Lord"* (Joshua 24:15).

So, go forward with courage, wisdom, and love! Be the difference that your family, your community, and this world so desperately need. And may the grace of the Lord Jesus Christ, the love of God, and the fellowship of the Holy Spirit be with you always.

Amen...

Date completed on this work: November 24th, 2024.

Tony Lynn Scott (Barnett)